Can Ye Feel So Now?

Simple Strategies to
Sustain Spiritual Strength

David T. Morgan, PhD

Published by David T. Morgan, PhD Inc Vancouver, Washington

CONTENTS

ACKNOWLEDGEMENTS

At the heart of this book is the idea that we can be changed by our experiences. Writing a book is always an interesting experience for me, one that usually results in greater personal insights and hard-fought spiritual change. After all, it's one thing to distribute advice to others; it is another thing entirely to follow it yourself. Because of the influence of others, I feel like I become better over time. My progress is often characterized as two steps forward and one step back, but overall the progress has been positive. I'm so thankful to my parents and siblings who have been a constant source of inspiration. Without exception, their lives have been touched by trial and difficulty and yet they have weathered the storms admirably. I love them very much.

So many have helped with manuscript reviews, critical analysis, proofreading, and overall emotional support. I'm grateful to Deena Morgan, Sharyle Karren, Janet Petersen, Dianne Esplin, Jeff Madsen, Marilyn Harker, Janae Smith, Barbara Rogers, Amy Morgan, and Sharon Cross for their selfless sacrifices of time and effort. I'm always grateful to my editor, Bonnie Brien, whose writing skills and talents have blessed me over and over. I'm thankful to Brad Wilcox for his helpful advice. Although I'll probably never be able to thank him in person, I'm grateful to Elder David A. Bednar who truly inspired so much of my thinking. I appreciate my children and grandchildren for their support and amazing examples. Finally, I'm forever thankful to my remarkable wife, Kristyn. I always tell her that she is the reason for everything good about me, and I mean it. Her example has helped me grow closer to my Savior, and I cannot express sufficient gratitude for that. She's simply the best.

PREFACE

I remember the day of my baptism. We lived in a small town in Wyoming and attended church in an old brick meetinghouse. I had been taught the gospel since I was young and understood the purpose of baptism. I knew the Lord would bless me for making a covenant with Him. As I came out of the water, I had a tremendous feeling of peace. I specifically remember thinking, "I never want to sin again." With all the sincerity my eight-year-old heart could produce, I left the church building that day with the goal to remain free of sin. Unsurprisingly, my resolve lasted for about ten minutes before I started an argument with my sister. My commitment to live a sinless life had been very short-lived. Although I didn't know it at the time, this experience was a prelude to the rest of my mortal journey.

Since then my spiritual life has been a voyage involving majestic peaks and miserable valleys. I have felt the Spirit in powerful measure, including moments where I have felt the Savior's love in a personal and meaningful way. I have experienced the sincere joy of forgiveness through the power of the Atonement of Jesus Christ. These times have been wonderful and life changing. On occasion I have felt so good that I never wanted to sin again. Other times I have felt the grief of straying from the path. I have endured temptations so strong that it seemed I could not resist. At other times I have wept inconsolably, feeling sorrow for sin. Because of the Savior's Atonement, *these difficult experiences have been wonderful and life changing as well.* Nevertheless, this "going back and forth" between periods of spiritual motivation and spiritual weakness worried me for many years. Why couldn't I just start my spiritual progression and never look back? Why not just go from baptism to temple marriage, constantly keeping my covenants, on an undeviating, upward trajectory?

With age and experience, I don't worry about these issues as much as before. First, I know that life is meant to be challenging. Our Father in Heaven knows we are going to fail on occasion. Because of this, He deliberately provided a Savior so we can repent and return to Him. Second, the grief of wandering can give way to the joy of redemption. "And it must needs be that the devil should tempt the children of men, or they could not be agents unto themselves; for if they never should have bitter they could not know the sweet" (D&C 29:39). Part of feeling the sweetness of obedience comes from having had the opposite experience of having gone astray. Nevertheless, there is always greater joy in following the commandments. One of the greatest lessons in life is to learn how to reduce periods of spiritual wandering and increase time staying faithful to God.

Perhaps your life has been similar. Perhaps you've had times when you've felt anything was possible through the power of the Atonement of Jesus Christ. Perhaps you've had other times when the thought of enduring a seemingly bleak future looked absolutely overwhelming. If so, this book is for you. Whether it is the soul-harrowing pain of sin (see Alma 36:12) or the scorching flames of trial and difficulty (see Isaiah 48:10), we all inevitably find ourselves at emotional low points in this life. When contrasted with spiritual highs, these experiences can feel particularly miserable. Nevertheless, our loving Father in Heaven has provided a pattern to guard against spiritual lows and to spend more time on the spiritual high ground. As you understand this pattern and adhere to the principles contained therein, you will more fully experience the joy that is the design of our existence (see 2 Nephi 2:25).

INTRODUCTION

Jesus Christ was the only perfect person to have ever lived on this earth. Everyone else will experience the grief of sin. "For all have sinned, and come short of the glory of God" (Romans 3:23). This means that all of us will disobey and taste the bitter. It also means that all of us will be able to have the wonderful experience of comparing the bitter to the sweet, learning to appreciate the marvelous difference.

As the father of five boys, I have participated in many outdoor activities. I've been on two high adventure activities, three scout camps, three pioneer treks, and more camping trips than I can recall. I don't particularly like camping, but I like spending time with my children. I would much rather be at home in my comfortable bed than on the cold ground in the wilderness. On one memorable camping trip, we traveled to higher elevations to build snow caves and sleep in them. While not thrilled about it, I went along without complaint. As we arrived at the campsite, there was enough snow to make things very cold, but not enough snow to build caves. Instead we pitched tents and turned in for the night. As I got ready for bed, I was absolutely freezing! What started with chattering teeth progressed to seizure-like convulsing. I truly cannot recall another time in my life when I was so cold. As I lay down to sleep on a *literal sheet of ice,* the only protection I had was a bargain sleeping bag atop an insufficient camping pad. That night was miserable.

Following the worst two hours of sleep ever, I arose in the morning and eventually returned home. Exhausted, I climbed into bed like I had done many times before. However, this experience was different. That bed felt more luxurious than I remembered. It was warm, cozy, soft; all the things that were absent the previous night. The nap that followed clearly ranks in the top ten most excellent naps I have ever had. I am confident the reason that nap was so great was because I had just come from a night of sleep that was so terrible. Having slept on ice made my bed feel that much more amazing.

Part of our mortal lives is to experience the negative so we can learn to prefer the good. We are truly dual beings. A portion of us is divine—our spirits are literally the offspring of heavenly parents. That celestial part of us yearns for connection to the eternal and wants to do what is right. On the other side, there is a portion of us that is corrupt. Because of the Fall of Adam, our originally pure spirits have been tainted with worldly cravings: "And he said unto them: Because that Adam fell, we are; and by his fall came death; and we are made partakers of misery and woe. Behold Satan hath come among the children of men, and tempteth them to worship him; and men have become carnal, sensual, and devilish, and are shut out from the presence of God" (Moses 6:48-49).

Thus we are left to choose between good and evil, having desires for both. Left to our own devices, chances are we'll choose evil more often than good. Our base natures tend to seek for immediate gratification, which is often in conflict with God's commands. However, with the refining and transforming power of the Holy Ghost, we can learn to choose good more often than evil. In His wisdom, our Heavenly Father makes the good appear desirable while leaving the enticements of evil firmly in place. Hence our choices between the two represent a true test of our resolve. Will we choose righteousness or wickedness? That is one of the great questions of life.

In His mercy, our Heavenly Father allows us to have grand spiritual experiences. During such times we feel His powerful love, and His influence in our lives is unmistakable. Consider some of the following scriptural examples:

- Lehi partakes of the fruit of the tree of life and is filled with the love of God.

- Abraham hears the voice of the angel, commanding him to not sacrifice Isaac.

- Helaman discovers that none of his stripling warriors have perished during a battle that claimed the lives of thousands of others.

- Grief-stricken Mary recognizes the voice of the resurrected Lord as He speaks her name in the garden.

- Faithful Nephites rejoice as they watch the sun go down, yet no darkness occurs; the foretold sign of the birth of Christ had finally happened.

Other spiritual experiences may not be on so grand a scale but have a similar significant impact. Consider some of these that you may have experienced:

- Witnessing the birth of a child or grandchild.

- Experiencing a missionary return home from faithful service.

- Seeing the baptism of a friend you introduced to the gospel.

- Feeling the power of testimony as you have received a witness of truth.

All such experiences are designed to give us a spiritual "reference point." Our Father in Heaven wants us to remember what it felt like to have that joy and happiness. When we wander from the path, He wants us to notice the difference between the feelings that come from straying and the feelings that come from obedience. That contrast is designed to motivate us to repent and try to regain the marvelous experiences felt during spiritual highs. The teaching of ancient and modern prophets provides practical, powerful counsel on how we can do this.

The title of this book promises "simple" strategies to help maintain spiritual power in our lives. I want to briefly explain the difference between "simple" and "easy," as I find that people often confuse the two. Simple is the opposite of complex. Simple tasks are those that are quickly understood, at least in how to execute them. Easy is the opposite of difficult. Simple tasks are not always easy. Moving a two-ton pile of rocks from one place to another is simple. All you need to do is take the rocks, a few at a time, and put them somewhere else. However, that task is very difficult because you are dealing with four thousand pounds of rocks. The suggested strategies in this book are designed to be simply understood. In most cases, however, they will be difficult to execute. Don't let this deter you. Difficult challenges can ultimately be the most rewarding. In addition, they have the potential to contribute to significant spiritual growth.

CHAPTER ONE

"We Went Forth Even in Wrath"

Alma the Younger was a powerful Book of Mormon prophet. He was the spiritual and secular leader of a difficult people. Yet prior to his conversion, he was wicked, actively seeking to destroy the church of God. Due to his father's faith and the Savior's mercy, he changed his life and went on to become an amazing witness of truth. Alma has a powerful backstory, one that seems to begin with the prophet Abinadi, even before Alma's birth. I love thinking about the men and women in the scriptures as the real, authentic people they truly were. It interests me to consider their strengths, weaknesses, and day-to-day struggles. Please permit me a bit of poetic license as I describe Alma the Younger's history through these hypothetical journals.

A Prophet's Journal

I am Abinadi. I was raised during the time of King Zeniff. He was a good man yet overeager to return to the land of our nativity, the land of Nephi. As that land was overrun with Lamanites, Zeniff had to enter into a treaty with their king to secure lands for our inheritance. Despite fair promises, things eventually devolved, and we had wars with the Lamanites to preserve our freedom. Zeniff eventually died and we are now under the rule of his son, King

Noah. I hesitate to even call him "king" because he is nothing like his father and hardly a good example. I have a bad feeling about where he will lead us...

...My fears have been confirmed; King Noah is a complete mess. He instituted a tax where we have to pay one-fifth of all our goods in order to support his laziness and debauchery. He abandoned the ways of his decent father, but even worse, he has abandoned the ways of the Lord. For me, I will continue to teach my family the truth and to look forward to the coming of the Messiah. If my fellow citizens follow King Noah, it will surely lead to their destruction, but it is not my place to intervene...

...Things have taken a dramatic turn. I was visited of the Lord and commanded to preach repentance to my people. Notwithstanding my weakness, I went and did so. They rejected me with forcefulness. It was as I feared; they fell in with King Noah's wicked traditions and now resist the call to repentance. They ultimately expelled me from the city and have forbidden me to return. For a moment I thought perhaps my mission was complete, but the Lord has counseled otherwise. I must return and preach the Lord's message regardless of who will follow. I don't feel like they will listen. I fear they will treat me harshly, and perhaps even follow through with their threats to end my life. But I know what I must do. Even if one person believes my message, my efforts will be worthwhile. I need to find a way to get back into the city to preach. Perhaps I should create a disguise...

A Priest's Journal

I am Alma the Elder. I am a powerful priest of the most honorable King Noah. We rule over this people in righteousness. There are some that claim we have strayed from the truth, but they are deceived. Men were created by God to be happy. We teach these people to enjoy their lives and do what they want. We are a free people and should not be held down by rules or commandments. Our people love and support us, and we gratefully accept their generous contributions as recompense for our hard and diligent work...

...I've just received word that the instigator Abinadi is once again preaching against King Noah. We had him thrown out of the city at one point; he must have snuck back in somehow. Abinadi is bold and accusatory. He has made public threats against the life of our great king, stating the Lord will destroy King Noah like a stiff breeze scatters dandelion thistle. The king has ordered his arrest and arraignment before our noble court. As the leaders of this people, we cannot tolerate such sedition. If he does not renounce what he has taught, we will very likely sentence him to death. It is the only reasonable course of action for traitors...

...Things have taken a dramatic turn. Abinadi was brought before us and the king ordered his execution. As the guards tried to take him, he was protected with divine power. The light of God seemed to shine from his face. He taught us mighty doctrine, the likes of which I had never heard before. My heart felt compelled to believe. I knew what he said was true. After he finished delivering his message the power of God departed from him. He was taken into custody. My fellow priests and I counseled together about what to do. I argued that his words were true, that we should let him go and seriously consider changing our ways. King Noah was enraged at my defense of Abinadi and cast me out, sending his guards to kill me. I was able to escape and am now in hiding, writing all of the words of Abinadi that I can recall. I don't know what they will do with me if they find me. I fear they may kill Abinadi, but even now I pray for his safety...

A Prodigal's Journal

My name is Alma. At church they call me "Alma the Younger" so I don't get confused with my lame dad. My dad makes me go to these really dumb activities for the boys my age. Tonight, they are making us write these stupid journals. The only reason I'm doing it is because I know that if I don't, my leaders will tell my dad, and then I'll get grounded or something worse. So, I'll write on this dumb scroll about my dumb life and how I can't wait to leave home so I can stop listening to all the lame lessons my dad gives about Jesus and church and blah blah blah blah...

...Now it's been a long time since I wrote anything, and I actually just found this scroll from that stupid young man activity some years ago. Dad is still doing his church stuff. In fact, he's the leader of the whole church now, which makes things even worse for me. But I've found a way to get back at him. One of the advantages to having a leader for a dad is that you get to hang out with other powerful people. I've found some good friends, four in fact; they are the sons of our king, King Mosiah. They feel the same way I do. They are sick and tired of hearing about church and sin and all of that nonsense. We've found there are many people in our community who believe as we do; they are tired of being preached at as well. We've started our own brand of preaching and actually have a decent following. If we can get enough of them on our side, we might just be able to bring down this entire church...

...Things have taken a dramatic turn. Our efforts to destroy the church enjoyed great success. As I traveled with the sons of Mosiah to continue our assault on the truth, we were confronted by an angel of God. I have never been more scared in my life. His voice shook the ground and every word he spoke sounded like thunder. He addressed me specifically, warning that I should stop trying to destroy the church of God. I fell unconscious and was out for three days. I remember that time; it seemed like three years. I felt tremendous remorse for what I had done, having led away innocent souls to destruction. In the throes of my agony, I remembered what my father had taught about repentance and forgiveness, through Jesus Christ. With deep sincerity, I pleaded to

God for relief. *In an instant*, my pain was gone. I saw the heavens opened and wanted to be there. From that time forward, I knew my mission. I had to undo the wrongs I had done. I had to preach the truth the rest of my days. I have since become the leader of the church, following in my amazing father's footsteps. But even now, the members of the church labor in wickedness. I've got my work laid out before me...

Consider the sequence of events that led to Alma the Younger's conversion. Abinadi chose to respond to the call to preach to a wicked people. His incredible bravery ensured the Lord's message was delivered to King Noah and his priests. The witness of the Holy Ghost led Alma the Elder to believe in Abinadi's words and teach them to others, including his family. Alma the Elder's faith led to the angel's intervention with his son. Alma the Younger's humility led to his repentance and the beginning of a life of Christlike service.

We know that Alma the Younger was a mighty preacher and had significant influence on the people. He gave amazing discourses to the church in Zarahemla and Gideon. His experiences with Amulek in the city of Ammonihah are incredible and a solid testimony of enduring faithfully through trials. Later in life he led another group of missionaries, this time including his own sons, to recover the apostate Zoramites. Having been a powerful political leader as the former chief judge of the people, Alma knew the influence an individual could have on thousands. Having been a warrior and personally fought in battles, he knew of the strength of physical force. Yet he also knew that the most powerful effect possible, one that would eclipse the law or the sword, was the word of God. "And now, as the preaching of the word had a great tendency to lead the people to do that which was just—yea, it had had more powerful effect upon the minds of the people than the sword, or anything else, which had happened unto them— therefore Alma thought it was expedient that they should try the virtue of the word of God" (Alma 31:5).

I believe one of the reasons Alma the Younger was such an amazing spiritual leader was because of his history. He had truly tasted the bitter and was able to clearly differentiate between the sting of sin and the reward of righteousness. If there was ever a prophet who was able to preach repentance with authenticity, it was Alma. His history prepared him to understand how to lead people to paths of happiness. As we study Alma's history and teachings in greater detail, we too can understand how to endure spiritual lows and return to spiritual highs. The following chapters explain these teachings and provide advice on how to remain on the covenant path.

Questions for self-reflection:

How have your challenges led to greater spiritual understanding?

Think about a particular difficulty in your life. Honestly evaluate: how would your life be better or worse without this trial?

What lessons is the Lord trying to teach you through your personal struggles?

CHAPTER TWO

"After Wading Through Much Tribulation"

Alma the Younger was on a collision course for destruction. He and the sons of Mosiah were determined to destroy the church their fathers had worked so hard to preserve. I can only imagine the grief their parents must have experienced. Surely many of us have had children who were wayward and disobedient at times, but how many can say their children have not only gone astray, but have then diligently tried to annihilate those things their parents held dear? These parents held out faithful, teaching truth and praying in faith that Father in Heaven would reach out to their children and help them see the error of their ways. Although not all parents of wayward children receive answers to prayer as they hope, God did answer the prayers of Alma the Elder and King Mosiah in a very dramatic fashion.

As Alma the Younger traveled with his delinquent companions, they were confronted by an angel. Sometimes angels come with good news, like Gabriel to Mary or Moroni to Joseph Smith. This angel came with a stern warning. His thunderous voice caused the ground under their feet to shake. Alma was the primary recipient of the message, as the angel commanded: "Alma, arise and stand forth, for why persecutest thou the church of God? For the Lord hath said: This is my church, and I will establish it;

and nothing shall overthrow it, save it is the transgression of my people" (Mosiah 27:13).

Mormon describes Alma the Younger as a "man of many words [who] did speak much flattery to the people" (Mosiah 27:8). There were many in the church who believed in Alma's deceptions and subsequently lost their faith. I'm sure Alma became somewhat convinced of his own persuasive abilities, thinking that through his efforts and skill he could accomplish his design of weakening or destroying the church. One of the challenges of being very good at something is we begin to believe we can do things on our own, as if heavenly help is not constantly necessary. Yet the angel's first admonition quickly established the relationship between Alma and God. The church Alma had targeted was God's church. Nothing would cause its failure except the iniquity of church members. In other words, Alma's flattering words and convincing speech would never destroy the church because God had ordained it so. Our Father in Heaven is in charge and nothing disrupts His eternal decrees, particularly the efforts of wayward mortals.

When I've taught about Alma the Younger, I've often asked class participants, "When the angel appeared to Alma, what did he command him to do?" Typically, most people say, "He told him to stop destroying the church." That is true. However, first, the angel invited Alma to *start* doing something instead of simply stopping his disobedient ways. The angel's injunction included the following: "Go, and *remember the captivity of thy fathers* in the land of Helam, and in the land of Nephi; and *remember how great things he has done for them*; for they were in bondage, and he has delivered them. And now I say unto thee, Alma, go thy way, and seek to destroy the church no more" (Mosiah 27:16, emphasis added). In other words, the angel said 1) remember the good things that have happened in your life and 2) stop destroying the church. We know that Alma ceased his efforts to thwart the growth of the church. But what of the first command, the one to remember the goodness of God? Did he follow through with this invitation as well?

Many years later, when Alma the Younger had adult children of his own, he gave counsel to his son Helaman. Among other things, Alma told him, "Yea, and he has also brought our fathers out of the land of Jerusalem; and he has also, by his everlasting power, delivered them out of bondage and captivity, from time to time even down to the present day; *and I have always retained in remembrance their captivity*; yea, and ye also ought to retain in remembrance, as I have done, their captivity" (Alma 36:29, emphasis added). Clearly, Alma had followed both angelic directives. One was relatively simple: he had to stop fighting the church. As far as we can tell, he stopped that the moment he awoke from his three-day coma. But the other command was much more difficult. He needed to regularly and consistently remember the history of his father's people, particularly how they were in bondage and how the Lord redeemed them. Their story of deliverance is remarkable and miraculous. For whatever reason, remembering this story would be critical to Alma's spiritual success. But why would the angel give such a command? How would it affect Alma's spiritual progression?

We can answer that question by examining our own lives and how "remembering" helps encourage obedience to God's commandments. A personal example may provide insight. Some time ago, we had a stake conference where Elder David A. Bednar of the Quorum of the Twelve Apostles presided. When I heard that he would be there, *in our stake center*, I was beyond excited. We don't typically get apostles at our stake conferences, so I knew it would be a once-in-a-lifetime experience. I was serving as elders quorum president and was invited to a four-and-a-half-hour group training with Elder Bednar on a Saturday morning. Under normal circumstances, I would not have been enthusiastic about such a long meeting, but this was different. We were given assigned seats and I was on the front row, just below the podium. I probably could have reached out and touched Elder Bednar with a decent stretch of the arm. For almost five hours, we sat and listened to his counsel, wisdom, and testimony. He let us ask questions. I was able to ask one and his answer helped me tremendously.

The next morning, we met again in the general session of stake conference. Elder Bednar spoke for a full hour and it was marvelous. Afterwards we talked with our children about their experience. Our seventeen-year-old son said, "That was the first church meeting I've ever been in that I didn't want to end." I felt the same way. For the next few weeks Elder Bednar's words were loud and clear in my thoughts. I reflected on them often, and his teachings helped me make better choices. Then things started to change a little. Work got busier and I found my thoughts turning more and more to employment responsibilities. One of our sons was getting ready to go to college for the first time and I began planning for that. Two of our children were in a high school theater production and we were busy helping them. Elder Bednar's teachings were less and less prominent in my mind. In fact, I found that unless I intentionally reflected on them, I could go days without thinking about what he taught. How could this be? This was a singular experience that truly changed my life, yet only weeks later I was having difficulty bringing it to the forefront of my mind.

I have found this is not an uncommon experience. I don't know why we have difficulty remembering influential moments, even powerful events. Sometimes I'll have an incredible experience and think, *there's no way I'll ever forget this.* Yet years later someone will ask about it and my recollection will be vague, if I recall it at all. Perhaps you have been through something similar. Our lives are full of distractions, both good and bad. We have a limited amount of mental energy, and when we use that energy for one thing, that means it is not available for another. When I try to actively remember the truths I learned from Elder Bednar, I feel spiritually strengthened and motivated. When I get distracted and lose focus on what he taught, I feel less inclined to follow his divine invitations to change.

It seems one of the reasons Alma the Younger was commanded to remember the captivity of his fathers was to help him remain humble and obedient. So how does this work? How does remembering certain events of the past help us have greater motivation to make good choices now? In Alma's case, he was asked to remember the account of the miraculous delivery of his father's people from enemy bondage. I presume as he reflected on this amazing story, it helped him realize the Lord's love for him and his dependence upon God. In turn, this helped him increase his desire to humbly follow heavenly direction. Remembering blessings and spiritual highlights can help us remain strong and motivated. Forgetting them can contribute to spiritual apathy. This phenomenon is exemplified by the following Book of Mormon account.

Samuel the Lamanite was an incredible ancient American prophet. Among other things, he prophesied both the birth and death of Jesus Christ, including the mighty acts of nature that would attend these respective phenomena. One of the signs of the birth of Christ would be unmistakable. There would be a day, a night, and a day without any darkness. The sun would set as usual, but it wouldn't get dark. This would be an unprecedented experience, so you can imagine the unbelievers were highly skeptical of this forecasted event. Those who believed in the words of Samuel looked forward to this future day with faith. Those who did not believe in Samuel's prophecy derided their associates and told them they were foolish to believe in such an unlikely and clearly impossible situation. In fact, the unbelievers were so frustrated with the faithful saints that they created a forecast of their own. They identified a future date when they would murder all believers if the so-called "heavenly sign" did not happen by then. Can you hear the words of these detractors? *You are fools to believe in Christ! You are even more foolish to believe that nature will somehow change her thousand-years' tradition of darkness at night. In fact, if your "sign" doesn't happen by the end of the month, we will kill you all.*

I have often reflected on how this circumstance would have impacted the believers. If you were a faithful saint, it would have been easy and very tempting to renounce your position and join with the unbelievers, if only to preserve your life and the life of your family. Perhaps some saints made this choice. Yet in my imagination I can see other saints who remained faithful despite the threats of death. They knew Samuel the Lamanite had spoken the truth. His words had been confirmed in their hearts through the power of the Holy Ghost. Each day they taught their children to believe and the Lord would deliver them. Each evening they would gather as families to watch the sunset. As the sun went down, their hearts would beat a little quicker as they thought, *Is tonight the night? Will the sign be given?* With each night that dusk gave way to darkness, their hearts sank. Yet they still had faith and said to each other: *Don't worry. It will happen someday. We have to believe.* With the date of their execution creeping closer by the day, each night of darkness likely brought increased fear but additional chances to exercise their faith.

I think one of the most thrilling events in scripture had to be the night when the sign was finally given. I imagine the faithful gathering again, as they had done for so many evenings. Perhaps their numbers were fewer as the days progressed. Yet there were still many who fixed their eyes on the horizon, the sun slowly setting, their hearts holding fast to faith and resisting fear. On that particular night, the usual time of dusk seemed different. It was still light. They may have thought, *it could just be a bright night.* Maybe they were hesitant to get their hopes up. But then the sun went down entirely, and the light remained. Perhaps they waited for another hour just to make sure. At some point it became obvious and they knew for certain that this was the long-promised time when Jesus would be born. Just as the heavenly sign was unmistakable for the believers, it was also unmistakable for the unbelievers. Not only had the unbelievers been wrong, it was now clear they had been in opposition to God's purposes. This caused them significant distress: "For behold, at the going down of the sun there was no darkness; and the people began to be astonished because there was no darkness when the night came. *And there were many, who had not believed the words of the prophets, who fell to the earth and became as if they were dead,* for they knew that the great plan of destruction which they had laid for those who believed in the words of the prophets had been frustrated; for the sign which had been given was already at hand" (3 Nephi 1:15-16, emphasis added).

What I find most interesting is what happened later. Satan had successfully deceived many unbelievers prior to the miraculous event. It was probably easy to convince them there would never be a night without darkness, which in turn meant Samuel the Lamanite was a liar, which in turn meant there would be no Christ. But after the light-filled night of Jesus' birth, there was no denying what had happened. Satan, now in damage-control mode, began to do what he could to reclaim his former unbelievers: "And it came to pass that from this time forth there began to be lyings sent forth among the people, by Satan, to harden their hearts, to the intent that they might not believe in those signs and wonders which they had seen; *but notwithstanding these lyings and deceivings the more part of the people did believe, and were converted unto the Lord*" (3 Nephi 1:22, emphasis added). Despite Satan's best efforts, the majority of people did not believe his lies. They had seen a miracle with their own eyes. They knew Samuel the Lamanite had spoken the truth. Their minds could not be altered. This was clearly a victory for heaven and a loss for hell, right? Well, let's look forward about five years and see what happened...

And it came to pass that thus passed away the ninety and fifth year also, and the people began to forget those signs and wonders which they had heard, and began to be less and less astonished at a sign or a wonder from heaven, insomuch that they began to be hard in their hearts, and blind in their minds, and began to disbelieve all which they had heard and seen— Imagining up some vain thing in their hearts, that it was wrought by men and by the power of the devil, to lead away and deceive the hearts of the people; and thus did Satan get possession of the hearts of the people again, insomuch that he did blind their eyes and lead them away to believe that the doctrine of Christ was a foolish and a vain thing. (3 Nephi 2:1-2)

Please permit me a personal rant. *Are you kidding me?? Just five years prior,* these people witnessed a miracle of unprecedented grandeur! They had never seen something so astounding in their entire lives. They literally sat on the ground, watched the sun go down, and yet there was noon-day brightness the entire night. Many of them even passed out due to their amazement. And yet, less than two thousand sunsets later, they doubted what they had seen with their own eyes. I'm sure many faithful saints continued to remember and believe what they saw. Their amazing experience that night became a spiritual witness and powerful testimony for the rest of their lives. But the unbelievers not only forgot their experience but also started to create fictions that perhaps the miracle was fabricated or maybe didn't even occur at all.

Does this account help you understand the power of remembering? Does it make sense why Alma the Younger was commanded to remember the captivity of his fathers? Do you see why we should remember the great things the Lord has done for us? In the account we just reviewed, those who remembered continued in paths of righteousness, while those who forgot or disbelieved wandered in sinful roads. When the angel commanded Alma to remember specific aspects of his history, this was to help him stay true to his beliefs and not be led astray by future temptations and deceptions. On several future occasions, Alma reiterated his commitment to remembering: "Yea, I have always remembered the captivity of my fathers; and that same God who delivered them out of the hands of the Egyptians did deliver them out of bondage" (Alma 29:12).

The Lord wants us to remember the blessings He has given us. As we choose to remember these things, we become humbler and more teachable. On the other hand, Satan wants us to forget our blessings yet recall our sins and missteps. He wants us to dwell on the negative aspects of our past, continually beating ourselves up for mistakes made days, weeks, months, and even years ago. While there can be tremendous value in learning from previous poor decisions, there is little to no value in carrying sinful burdens where repentance is complete. Try not to get caught in this trap. Satan is the great counterfeiter; if remembering and dwelling upon good things is a powerful tool for forward progress, then remembering and dwelling upon bad things can be a potent tool to keep us stuck.

If you find yourself weighed down with the burden of past sins, reflect upon one of the Lord's many statements regarding repentance: "Behold, he who has repented of his sins, the same is forgiven, and I, the Lord, remember them no more" (D&C 58:42). We won't go into the details of proper repentance here, but the doctrine of forgiveness is clear. When we truly repent, the Lord does not remember our sins. I think this is one of the most merciful doctrines in scripture. While Satan would have us rehash and relive every poor decision, constantly weighing us down with regret and shame, the Lord graciously forgives and "remembers them no more."

Alma the Younger found that remembering the Lord's grace helped him stay focused on his covenants and not get distracted by Lucifer's clever diversions. Surely Alma could have been hampered by thoughts of his past sinful life, but I don't believe he let this become a burden. He remembered the good, rejected the bad, and moved forward with faith. This example is key in helping us develop the ability to remain spiritually strong during times of difficulty. We will all have spiritual highlights; keeping them fresh in our memory is key. Documenting our thoughts and feelings shortly after powerful spiritual experiences can help us remember them later. We can refer to them when we feel spiritually weak. We can allow the memory of powerful spiritual experiences to buoy us up. In addition, we can resist the memory of past poor choices to drag us down. This process is key to maintaining spiritual strength over time.

Questions for self-reflection:

What are some powerful spiritual experiences you have had?

Do you find it challenging to remember the good things the Lord has done for you? Why or why not?

How can remembering your blessings help you maintain spiritual strength?

CHAPTER THREE

"Behold I am Born of the Spirit"

Alma the Younger had probably never had a mightier spiritual manifestation than when he was confronted by the angel. After years of questioning, scoffing at his father's teachings, and active attempts to destroy the work of God, he was literally leveled to the ground with proof positive that his previous paths were wrong. The experience was so powerful that he lay unconscious for three days following the heavenly visit. The sons of Mosiah, who were his companions, took Alma's inert body to his father. Under most circumstances, if your son's delinquent friends dragged his body back to your house, you would probably be horrified. But Alma the Elder had the opposite reaction. He knew his prayers had been answered and the Lord had intervened.

After three comatose days, Alma the Younger awoke. Surely his father was very curious to hear what he would say. Did the angelic intervention work? Or was Alma the same, rebellious person he had been three days prior? His curiosity didn't last long, as Alma immediately spoke as follows: "I have repented of my sins, and have been redeemed of the Lord; behold I am born of the Spirit. And the Lord said unto me: Marvel not that all mankind, yea, men and women, all nations, kindreds, tongues and people, must be born again; yea, born of God, changed from their carnal and fallen state, to a state of righteousness, being redeemed of

God, becoming his sons and daughters. And thus they become new creatures; and unless they do this, they can in nowise inherit the kingdom of God" (Mosiah 27:24-26).

The concept of being "born again" is common among Christianity. But what does it really mean? We are all familiar with our first birth, the event that brought us into mortality. With that first breath, we began our path through life. We were transformed from just being a spirit to becoming a complete soul, the unity of spirit and flesh (see D&C 88:15). So, with that first birth, was everything complete? Had we finished our mortal purpose? Of course not! That event was the very beginning. Months, years, and decades of progress, change, and trials were to follow. No reasonable person would presume that the act of physical birth is the culminating event of mortality. On the contrary; although it is an essential part of life, it is completely insufficient to achieve our life's purposes.

So it is with our second birth, our spiritual rebirth. As Alma the Younger taught, everyone must experience another birth, being born of God. The reason we need this second birth is because we came from our heavenly abode into a fallen world. While our spirits may have been obedient in our former home, our bodies often have different agendas. In the pre-mortal existence, we thrilled at the promise that we would obtain physical bodies and become like our Father in Heaven. Yet I don't think we knew just how difficult the management of these bodies would be. At some point in our lives we all become acquainted with the "natural man." The natural man represents our base, inappropriate, and unrestrained desires (see Mosiah 3:19). In my mind's eye I picture this meeting of spiritual and natural selves. My spiritual self is dressed in a suit, holding a copy of the scriptures, and is eager to do well. As I walk around the corner, I see a seedy individual leaning against the wall. He looks just like me. He is wearing torn jeans and a t-shirt that says "carnal, sensual, devilish, and proud of it." His whole being exudes a shifty and shady attitude. As I try to walk past him, we have the following interaction:

Natural me: "Hold on there, where are you going?"

Spiritual me: "I'm going to church. Surely *you* have no idea where to find it, so I'll just be on my way, thank you very much."

Natural me: "I'm coming with you."

Spiritual me: "Seriously? You want to go to church??"

Natural me: "Not remotely. But I'll be going with you wherever you go. You see, we are a package deal. You come to earth, you get the natural man. I've just become your constant companion. So yeah, let's go to church. Maybe I can find a meeting to sleep through."

And thus begins one of the greatest challenges of our mortal experience: being constantly torn between our spiritual desires and our natural instincts. If you haven't figured it out already, *the natural man is a drag.* He is a pain in the rear. His goals are completely inconsistent with our desires to return to Heavenly Father. At the same time, his role is absolutely essential in our lives. Lehi taught his son Jacob that opposition is critical to the plan of salvation: "For it must needs be, that there is an opposition in all things. If not so, my firstborn in the wilderness, righteousness could not be brought to pass, neither wickedness, neither holiness nor misery, neither good nor bad" (2 Nephi 2:11). This makes sense; how could we know truth if we didn't know deception? The sweet becomes that much more desirable after having experienced the bitter.

While the natural man may want to be our constant companion, we have a choice in the matter. We are invited to replace his continuous company with the high-caliber companionship of the Holy Ghost. This is a core feature of spiritual rebirth. Just like our mortal birth changed us from spirit form to physical form, spiritual birth is designed to change us from natural and sinful to spiritual and holy. How does this process happen? For some, they have a single, significant moment where a powerful spiritual manifestation marks the beginning of their spiritual journey. For most others, the beginning is more mundane. Let's consider an example of each.

Just prior to his death, King Benjamin gave an incredible sermon to his people (see Mosiah, chapters three through five). He outlined the horrible realities of physical and spiritual death. He taught the saints that without some sort of intervention, they would all be miserably and hopelessly lost forever. Then he preached the truth of the coming Messiah, who would vanquish death for all and provide escape from sin upon conditions of repentance. The people thrilled to understand this concept. Yet at the same time, they felt guilty for their sins. They wanted mercy. They all cried to God and immediately received peace and forgiveness. This must have been a powerful spiritual moment. Later in his discourse, King Benjamin asked the people if they believed what he had taught them. They reported, "Yea, we believe all the words which thou hast spoken unto us; and also, we know of their surety and truth, because of the Spirit of the Lord Omnipotent, *which has wrought a mighty change in us*, or in our hearts, that we have no more disposition to do evil, but to do good continually" (Mosiah 5:2, emphasis added). This experience was surely akin to a spiritual rebirth, changing them from natural men and women to men and women of Christ. It appears their change was so powerful they had no more desire to sin; how amazing!

My own spiritual journey has been far less spectacular than that of King Benjamin's people, but I clearly remember where it started. I grew up in a Latter-day Saint home. I was baptized at eight years of age, received the Aaronic priesthood at age twelve, and moved from office to office in that priesthood. I attended seminary, church, Young Men's activities, Scouts, and most other things you would expect with a typical adolescent Latter-day Saint boy. But I don't believe I had a testimony of the truth. I believed my parents knew it was true. I believed my seminary teachers knew it was true. I believed my bishop knew it was true. But I didn't know for myself. Quite frankly, I don't remember having the desire to know for myself. Relying on the testimony of others was sufficient for me, or so I thought.

After high school graduation, I went to Brigham Young University, planning to attend for one year and then serve a mission. I'm not sure how I thought I was going to be an effective missionary without a testimony of my own. My parents, seminary teachers, and bishop were not going on the mission with me. I think I had not thought that far in advance. Nevertheless, the Lord had other plans and mercifully intervened despite my cluelessness. I clearly remember sitting in sacrament meeting my freshman year at BYU. It was fast Sunday and I was listening to the bearing of testimonies. One of my peers went to the pulpit. I didn't know him. As I recall, his testimony was nice but nothing remarkable. It was the sort of thing I had heard hundreds of times over the course of my life. Yet when he bore witness of the divine calling of the prophet Joseph Smith, something rang especially true to me. The Spirit testified to me, in no uncertain terms, that Joseph Smith was God's prophet. Unlike the people of King Benjamin, I did not have an immediate and mighty change. But I felt like I had taken the first step on a journey that would lead to my own spiritual transformation.

It has been over thirty years since that experience, and it remains the cornerstone of my testimony. For me, spiritual change has been slow and somewhat steady. My life has been typical of most: striving to do what is right, failing in my attempts, repenting, being forgiven, and then back to striving. My testimony has grown little by little over the years. If that moment at BYU was the seed of truth and the beginning of my personal witness, then that seed has since grown to a towering tree of absolute certainty. That tree has grown like all trees do, little by little, benefitting from careful attention and regular nurturing. If I neglect the tree it will die, but if I continually provide needed sustenance it will remain forever. I believe that my spiritual rebirth started in that humble sacrament meeting, and much like my mortal birth and subsequent life, I have spiritually grown slowly and steadily since that time.

I've heard people comment how they wish they could be like Alma the Younger or the people of King Benjamin. They want to have one powerful spiritual experience that will set them on an unending path of righteousness once and for all. First, I don't believe that either Alma or King Benjamin's subjects were magically changed in the moment. I think that was the *beginning* of their spiritual journey, followed by many years of striving and determination. It seems contrary to life's purposes to have a single experience that provides unending and sufficient spiritual power for exaltation. I have found that the daily struggle, although difficult and tiresome, is absolutely essential in helping us meet the measure of our creation.

I have a friend who recently competed in an Ironman event. For those who don't know, the Ironman is one of the most grueling and physically-demanding challenges one can participate in. It begins with a 2.4 mile swim in open water, then moves immediately to a 112 mile bicycle ride, and culminates with a full marathon, which is 26.2 miles. It requires months and months of intense physical training. My friend chronicled his preparation on social media, and I got to follow along with his efforts from the comfort of my couch. After his extensive and diligent work, he was ready to compete. As I reflected on this, I thought, "What if he could have taken a pill that would have completely transformed his physical body, regardless of its current condition, rendering him totally fit and ready, and then competed and won the event?" The "pill" solution would have only taken an afternoon. He could have gone from the couch to the race in 24 hours and completely crushed the competition. In the post-race interview, he could have said, "I'd like to thank the makers of the Ironman Ready pill. The two minutes it took me to swallow that pill are some of the sweetest of my life; I'll never forget the journey."

Not only is that situation impossible, *it's not even desirable.* My friend ran the race. He did not finish first, but he finished successfully. It was one of the greatest accomplishments of his life. As he reflected on his efforts, he was filled with pride and gratitude. *Finishing* the race was sweet, but it was the *journey* that transformed him. Not only did he meet a personal goal and develop exceptional physical strength and endurance, but he also developed spiritual skills of motivation, diligence, sacrifice, determination, and so many others that he built over the course of months and years of preparation. The day will come when my friend will no longer be physically able to compete in such an event. But with ongoing discipline, he will always retain the spiritual skills he developed, throughout this life and into the next.

So often we see the destination as the goal. But the longer I live, the more I realize that the journey is most critical. Destinations come and go. Once you reach one, there is another looming in the distance. You typically don't stay at the destination for long. You might pause and survey the terrain, but then you are right back on the path toward the next goal. If arriving at destinations is your life's joy, you are likely to find little enjoyment overall. Instead, if we focus on the journey, finding happiness in day-to-day efforts to move forward, we'll experience more consistent joy.

With that understanding, let's discuss further the concept of spiritual rebirth, not as a single event but as an ongoing process. I suppose many of us might be able to identify the time when our spiritual rebirth began, but if we don't continue on the path after that moment, that event will have little lasting power. Elder David A. Bednar stated, "Spiritual rebirth...does not occur quickly or all at once; it is an ongoing process—not a single event. Line upon line and precept upon precept, gradually and almost imperceptibly, our motives, our thoughts, our words, and our deeds become aligned with the will of God. This phase of the transformation process requires time, persistence, and patience." [1]

---

1   David A. Bednar, "Ye Must Be Born Again," *Ensign*, May 2007, 21.

Doctrinally, the formal beginning of spiritual rebirth is baptism and confirmation. The Savior taught Nicodemus, "Except a man be born of water and of the Spirit, he cannot enter into the kingdom of God" (John 3:5). When we are baptized by proper priesthood authority, we make sacred covenants with Father in Heaven. Among other things, we agree to take upon us the name of Jesus Christ. Following baptism, we are confirmed members of the Church of Jesus Christ of Latter-day Saints. In that sacred ordinance, we obtain the gift of the Holy Ghost, which is the promise of His constant companionship if we are faithful. The authorized person performing the confirmation says the words, "Receive the Holy Ghost," and thus it is official. This is the beginning of spiritual rebirth. What is next?

Some time ago I was in church, preparing to partake of the sacrament. I listened to the sacramental prayer and something caught my ear like it hadn't before. "That they are *willing* to take upon them the name of thy Son" (D&C 20:77; emphasis added). It was the word "willing" that stood out to me. I thought about it. At first it seemed like an unnecessary request. Was I willing to take upon me the name of Jesus Christ? Of course! I mean, hadn't I done that almost forty years prior when I was baptized? Wasn't almost everyone in that church congregation baptized as well, and therefore had taken upon them His name? Why would the Lord want to know if I was willing to do something that I had already done? The willingness seemed implicit.

As I thought about it more deeply, I was impressed with a new interpretation. It was like the Spirit was saying, "David, of course I know you were willing to take upon you the name of the Savior when you were baptized. I was there and your young heart was eager to do so. What I want to know is, are you *still* willing to take His name upon you today? For this coming week, will you act as He would act? Speak as He would speak? Serve as He would serve? I'm not talking about choices made so many years ago; I'm talking about where you are *right now*. What is your willingness today?" That bit of instruction was astounding to me. It changed the way I viewed the sacrament. I was not simply attesting to a decades-old promise, but was *actively making* that promise again. Although spiritual rebirth may begin at baptism, it continues constantly through ongoing choices to do what is right.

The gift of the Holy Ghost has a similar application. As noted previously, we are commanded to "receive" the Holy Ghost upon confirmation. I had always thought that meant we opened some sort of door to our spiritual home, He walked in and found an empty bedroom, and stayed there. Yet I always knew that the presence of the Holy Ghost in my life was contingent on my obedience. Then a Book of Mormon scripture helped me achieve even greater insight into how receiving the Holy Ghost is a process and not an event. Amulek taught, "And now, my beloved brethren, I desire that ye should remember these things, and that ye should work out your salvation with fear before God, and that ye should no more deny the coming of Christ; *that ye contend no more against the Holy Ghost, but that ye receive it*" (Alma 34:37-38, emphasis added).

With that additional understanding, "receiving the Holy Ghost" seemed like an active, daily decision as opposed to something I obtained while simply sitting quietly with hands placed on my head. I especially appreciated Amulek's concept of "contending against the Holy Ghost" and how receiving it is the opposite. How many times have I sat in a comfortable chair and had an impression to get up and do something for someone? How often have I rationalized away such promptings, choosing comfort over sacrifice? For me, and I presume for many others, "contending against the Holy Ghost" is probably that common. Generally speaking, faithful members of the Church of Jesus Christ of Latter-day Saints are not rebellious. However, we are weak and prone to avoid needful action in favor of convenience. When we fail to act on heavenly invitations, we don't allow the Holy Ghost to influence and refine our lives. "Receiving the Holy

Ghost" needs to be a daily experience, constantly listening to promptings and choosing to follow them. Similar to being willing to take upon us the Savior's name, we have to receive the Holy Ghost on an ongoing basis.

Being born again thus becomes a daily, active process that involves continual choices and sacrifices. Instead of viewing this as a chore, I see it as a wonderful opportunity! The Lord knows that training for the race will bring much greater blessings than simply running it. By the same token, He knows that daily choices over a lifetime will bring greater spiritual growth than a single, amazing transcendent event. In the case of Alma the Younger, he experienced the commencement of his spiritual rebirth in mighty fashion. The true test happened every day for the rest of his life, just as it does for us. As with Alma, our spiritual rebirth not only has a beginning but is also a daily process of choosing to follow the Savior, repenting when we don't, and becoming more and more sanctified through the continual reception of the Holy Ghost.

Questions for self-reflection:

What events and experiences have contributed to your spiritual rebirth?

What aspects of the "natural man" do you find particularly challenging in your life?

What changes do you need to make to be ever "willing" to take upon you the name of Christ and to constantly "receive" the Holy Ghost in your life?

CHAPTER FOUR

"Have Ye Experienced This Mighty Change in Your Hearts?"

There's no question that Alma the Younger's conversion began in a dramatic and miraculous manner. He continued faithful for the rest of his life. Some might say, "Of course he remained faithful; how could you forget such an incredible experience?" Unfortunately, the scriptures have many examples of people who have had such amazing manifestations, then have discounted or forgotten them. We have already talked about the Nephites who after only five years stopped believing in the sign of Christ's birth. Here are just a few additional examples:

- The children of Israel witness the Red Sea part before their eyes, and not long after resort to worshiping a false god.

- Laman and Lemuel literally see an angel who tells them they will be successful in obtaining the plates of brass, then just moments later they express doubts they will be able to accomplish the task.

- The Jews witness multiple miracles performed by the Savior and then demand His crucifixion.

It seems that miracles and heavenly visits do not have unilateral power to convert people. However, such experiences create a fork in our spiritual path. Some choose to repent and pursue righteousness, while others choose to continue in paths of apathy or wickedness. What makes the difference?

Alma the Younger came to a similar spiritual fork in the road and chose righteousness. He and the sons of Mosiah had greatly disrupted the church in prior years. Following the angelic visit, they were faced with the prospect of trying to undo the damage they had caused. To their credit, they did not shy away from this daunting task but went to work. "And they traveled throughout all the land of Zarahemla, and among all the people who were under the reign of king Mosiah, zealously striving to repair all the injuries which they had done to the church, confessing all their sins, and publishing all the things which they had seen, and explaining the prophecies and the scriptures to all who desired to hear them" (Mosiah 27:35).

Following the death of his father, Alma the Younger became the prophet and leader of the Lord's church. In addition, he became the first chief judge of the newly-reorganized Nephite government. He was the religious and political leader of the Nephites and had tremendous responsibility. It was probably hard enough to bear such a heavy load without additional distractions, but Alma was confronted with a number of serious challenges during this time. In an ironic turn of events, Alma confronted a silver-tongued detractor who convinced many church members that obedience to commandments was not necessary and they should do what they want (see Alma 1:1-15). Alma's political status was challenged by a rebel group who wanted to undo the Nephite democracy and return to a system of kings. This led to a division among the people and ultimately civil war, where Alma himself fought in battle (see Alma 2-3).

The Nephites suffered tremendous loss during this war, which encouraged their humility. As they humbled themselves, they became more obedient. As they were obedient, they were blessed and prospered by the Lord. And as is shown over and over in Nephite history, prosperity led to pride and disobedience. "For [Alma] saw and beheld with great sorrow that the people of the church began to be lifted up in the pride of their eyes, and to set their hearts upon riches and upon the vain things of the world, that they began to be scornful, one towards another, and they began to persecute those that did not believe according to their own will and pleasure" (Alma 4:8).

Even worse, missionary work was thwarted by the poor behavior of church members. As you can imagine, it was difficult to encourage people to join a church where the members themselves were proud, boastful, and inconsiderate of others. Alma the Younger determined that he needed to devote himself full-time to the affairs of the church. He abdicated his political role as chief judge and committed all of his resources to serve as the prophet. He embarked on a tour of the land, preaching to church members in various cities, doing what he could to help them correct their evil ways and return to keeping their covenants. His first discourse was to the saints in Zarahemla, contained in Alma chapter five.

I find it interesting that Alma the Younger did not begin his Zarahemla sermon with a recitation of his conversion story. You'd think that would be a good opener, full of drama and likely to be very engaging to his audience. Instead, he discusses the history of his people, particularly their being in bondage to the Lamanites many years earlier. He then asks the people if they themselves have remembered the experiences of their forebears. That is precisely what the angel commanded Alma to do: to remember the good things the Lord had done for his fathers, especially in delivering them from bondage. This must have made a deep impression on Alma, encouraging his humility as he considered past blessings. Perhaps he hoped it would have the same effect on the Zarahemla saints, who clearly needed additional humility.

In noting the necessary transformation that comes through spiritual rebirth, Alma the Younger states, "And now behold, I ask of you, my brethren of the church, have ye spiritually been born of God? Have ye received his image in your countenances? Have ye experienced this mighty change in your hearts?" (Alma 5:14). These are excellent questions. As we have previously reviewed, spiritual rebirth is a lifelong process, but must start somewhere. I believe Alma's question refers to the beginning of that path. Alma's father needed the words of Abinadi to initiate his change. Alma the Younger needed the angel's visit to commence his transformation. Everyone needs to start somewhere, and Alma is simply asking his people if they have started their own spiritual journey.

There is another important aspect to Alma the Younger's questions. In the third one he posed: "Have ye experienced this mighty change in your *hearts*?" (Alma 5:14, emphasis added). Why didn't he ask if they had experienced the change in their minds? Why use the word "heart" to talk about this process of spiritual rebirth? As with almost any verse of scripture, I believe the wording is completely intentional. Often times, when moving from one decision to another, we talk about "changing our mind." For example, *I was going to go for a walk, but when I saw it was raining, I changed my mind.* It would seem strange to say, *I was going to go for a walk, but when I saw it was raining, I changed my heart.* There is a difference between the two statements. What is the difference between changing your mind and changing your heart?

Most information we receive is first processed by our mind, or our brain. It is a cognitive exercise where we understand and assimilate new knowledge. I think most spiritual information is received in the same way. I learned the story of the First Vision many years before the time I gained a testimony that Joseph Smith was a prophet. Before my testimony developed, I didn't doubt the facts I had learned. I understood that Joseph saw God the Father and Jesus Christ. If you had asked me about it, I could have recited the story with decent accuracy. Yet I didn't have a personal conviction that the story was true. Now, years later and many spiritual manifestations since, I *know* that Joseph Smith was a prophet of God. I can still recite the events of the First Vision. But I can also bear solemn witness that *it is true*. I believe my conviction regarding those events has traveled from my mind to my heart.

Paul wrote to the Corinthians, "Forasmuch as ye are manifestly declared to be the epistle of Christ ministered by us, written not with ink, but with the Spirit of the living God; not in tables of stone, *but in fleshy tables of the heart*" (2 Corinthians 3:3, emphasis added). The prophet Jeremiah recorded, "But this shall be the covenant that I will make with the house of Israel; After those days, saith the Lord, I will put my law in their inward parts, *and write it in their hearts*; and will be their God, and they shall be my people" (Jeremiah 31:33, emphasis added). Both of these scriptures suggest that true conversion is more than just understanding a gospel principle, but somehow being able to incorporate that principle at a deep, spiritual level, leading to a strength of testimony that motivates righteous choices. Sister Linda K. Burton, former Relief Society general president, stated, "When each of us has the doctrine of the Atonement written deep in our hearts, then we will begin to become the kind of people the Lord wants us to be when He comes again. He will recognize us as His true disciples…. Making, keeping, and rejoicing in our covenants will be the evidence that the Atonement of Jesus Christ is truly written in our hearts."[2]

When Alma the Younger spoke of having a mighty change of heart, I think that is exactly what he meant. "Mighty changes of mind" don't have near as much spiritual power as changes that occur in the heart. I'm sure that most Christians have all sorts of true beliefs, with some planted in their minds and some planted in

2   Linda K. Burton, "Is Faith in the Atonement of Jesus Christ Written in our Hearts?" *Ensign*, November 2012, 114.

their hearts. One of the key responsibilities of this life is to move those spiritual truths, little by little, from our minds to our hearts. Once they are planted in our hearts, they are likely to remain, especially if they are regularly nurtured. Alma provided counsel to the people of Zarahemla regarding how to do this, and his advice is instructive to us all.

An Eye of Faith

Alma the Younger posed another question to his group of wayward saints: "Do ye exercise faith in the redemption of him who created you? Do you look forward with an eye of faith, and view this mortal body raised in immortality, and this corruption raised in incorruption, to stand before God to be judged according to the deeds which have been done in the mortal body?" (Alma 5:15). Alma invited the people to peer into the future, imagining themselves reunited with Heavenly Father and being accountable for their choices. He then asked them to consider this situation a little further: "I say unto you, can you imagine to yourselves that ye hear the voice of the Lord, saying unto you, in that day: Come unto me ye blessed, for behold, your works have been the works of righteousness upon the face of the earth?" (Alma 5:16).

Many years ago, I was teaching an adult Sunday School class. I asked for a show of hands regarding who in the class believed they would someday be in the celestial kingdom. About a third of the class raised their hands, and about half of those with raised hands seemed only moderately convinced of their opinion. I was shocked. I don't recall the point of the lesson or what was subsequently discussed, but after these many years I still recall that particular moment. I was personally acquainted with most everyone in that class. They were good members of the Church of Jesus Christ of Latter-day Saints. They served in their callings, took care of each other, and strived to do what was right. In my estimation, every one of them was on target to achieve celestial glory if they maintained their trajectory. So why were so many of them evidently unconvinced of what I believed they were capable of?

In many cases, we are harder on ourselves than we are on anyone else. If someone else gives a mediocre performance on a project, the compassionate side of us will often say, "Oh, I'm sure they tried their hardest and did their best. What they did is just fine." Yet when we have the same unexceptional outcome from our own efforts, we tend to be more critical of ourselves and believe we should have been more dedicated or disciplined. I'll bet that if I had changed my question to the Sunday School class and asked, "How many of you think everyone else in this class will go to the celestial kingdom?" everyone would have raised their hands. Fortunately, we are not our own or each other's judges. No unfair bias will be applied at the final judgment. As Alma already noted, each of us will stand before God and His judgment will be merciful and fair.

Let me give you a little preview of what I believe the faithful are likely to experience in that moment of judgment. You will arrive at the judgment bar. You'll see your Father in Heaven and have an explosion of memories. You'll remember the times you spent with Him before you came to earth. You'll recall the wonderful talks you had together and the things He taught you. You will feel intense love for Him and want nothing more than to fully enter His presence. Then you'll have another set of memories. You'll think about the missteps you made in mortality. You'll consider the sinful behaviors you were never able to fully conquer despite your best efforts. Those feelings may create a sense of doubt, even panic. How will you be able to return to your loving Heavenly Father's presence if you are still unclean?

What is likely to follow next will probably be the greatest moment of your existence. You'll see another person, one who you immediately recognize. It is your Savior, Jesus Christ. With desperate consideration and tear-filled eyes, you'll look to Him.

You'll know what you want to ask but wonder if you even should. You'll want to access His atoning power to cleanse you and therefore permit the long-anticipated reunion with your Father. Before you can even speak, the Lord, your Advocate, will speak for you. "Father, behold the sufferings and death of him who did no sin, in whom thou wast well pleased; behold the blood of thy Son which was shed, the blood of him whom thou gavest that thyself might be glorified; Wherefore, Father, spare these my brethren that believe on my name, that they may come unto me and have everlasting life" (D&C 45:4-5). Of course Father in Heaven will agree, our cleansing will be complete, and through the blood of the Lamb we will rush to embrace our Heavenly Father, having the most joyous reunion imaginable.

Does that scenario give you hope? It should. When I think about that future day, my heart thrills with the possibility. As my faith in Jesus Christ deepens, that "possibility" seems more and more like a certain eventuality. I'm not trying to be proud or boastful, nor overestimate my potential to be redeemed. I believe this amazing situation is equally likely to all who exercise faith and strive to keep their covenants. I am acutely aware of my flaws and know that I will appear before the judgment bar with plenty of mortal stain. But I also believe that my Savior loves me, that He is compassionate and merciful, and that if I do my best to serve Him, notwithstanding my weakness, He will rescue me as promised.

Alma the Younger invites us all to look forward with the "eye of faith." The eye of faith looks forward with hope, trust, and eager anticipation. It helps us see an amazing future that is possible through faith in Jesus Christ and repentance. I suppose that Satan, that great fraud, would invite us to look forward with the "eye of doubt." The eye of doubt sees with pessimism, doom, and ultimate failure. *Don't buy Satan's lies.* As you look toward the future with happiness and determination, you will experience greater conversion. You will deepen your understanding of the Atonement of Jesus Christ and come to know Him better. Those true principles you currently understand in your mind will move to your heart, bringing a greater sense of determination and purpose.

The Image of God

Alma the Younger made an additional inquiry to the Zarahemla saints: "I say unto you, can ye look up to God at that day with a pure heart and clean hands? I say unto you, can you look up, having the image of God engraven upon your countenances?" (Alma 5:19). What does it mean to have the image of God engraven upon our countenances? President Russell M. Nelson provided some thoughts on this: "Each member can be an example of the believers.... As followers of Jesus Christ, each of you can live in accord with His teachings. You can have 'a pure heart and clean hands'; you can have 'the image of God engraven upon your [countenance].' Your good works will be evident to others. The light of the Lord can beam from your eyes." [3]

Sometimes I think we forget that we have godly potential. We are here to become like our heavenly parents. The process of transformation from what we are now to what we are invited to become is often misunderstood. We have the opportunity to develop a godlike character while still in this life, which involves much more than narrowly making the cut for entrance into the celestial kingdom. There are many things to learn and skills to develop. The more we learn and change in this life, the more advantage we will have in the life to come (see D&C 130:18-19). Joseph Smith taught that progress in this life is critical for our spiritual development, but there is more growth to experience after death:

> When you climb up a ladder, you must begin at the bottom, and ascend step by step, until you arrive at the top; and so it is with the principles of the gospel—you

---

3   Russell M. Nelson, "Be Thou An Example of the Believers." *Ensign*, November 2010, 48.

must begin with the first, and go on until you learn all the principles of exaltation. But it will be a great while after you have passed through the veil before you will have learned them. It is not all to be comprehended in this world; it will be a great work to learn our salvation and exaltation even beyond the grave. [4]

One of Jesus' parables can help us understand the importance of developing a heavenly character. Matthew chapter 20 details the account of the laborers in the vineyard. The parable begins by describing a man who owned a vineyard and needed help with its care. As such, he went out to hire laborers. At daybreak, he found workers and hired them for one penny a day. At the third hour, which would be about 9:00 a.m. in modern times, the man needed more help and hired more workers, for the same price. He did the same at the sixth and ninth hours. Then, at the eleventh hour, which would have been probably one hour before sundown and the end of the workday, the man hired even more laborers, promising them a penny as well.

When the workday ended, the master gathered the laborers and paid them according to their agreement: each of them a penny. As you can imagine, when those who had worked since sunrise saw they received the same payment as those who had worked for only an hour, they were upset. The owner of the vineyard corrected them, saying they had been dealt with fairly and given what they were owed. He further stated, "Is it not lawful for me to do what I will with mine own?" (Matthew 20:15). I think that is another way of saying, "It's my vineyard; it's my money; you are simply the hired help. If you don't like the wage, then don't take the job. But don't complain about my hiring practices when you are clearly not in a position to do so."

I used to feel that the all-day laborers were somehow slighted. As I have come to understand this parable in a different light,

---

4   Joseph Smith, *Teachings of the Presidents of the Church: Joseph Smith* (Salt Lake City: The Church of Jesus Christ of Latter-day Saints, 2007) 268.

I don't feel that way any longer. To my estimation, the master is the Savior and we are the laborers. The penny represents the ultimate gift, which is to return to God and live with Him forever. Everyone who abides by the conditions the Savior has established is entitled to the promised reward. That does *not* mean each person will experience an equal amount of work, sacrifice, repentance, or suffering. The paths we take to return to Father in Heaven are as individual as we are. Some will suffer with wayward children while others will not. Some will deal with chronic poverty and others will not. In essence, some will probably labor harder and longer to achieve the celestial kingdom than others will, like those who worked twelve hours versus one. Yet each of us has arranged our own individual deal with the Savior and He will honor the terms if we do our part.

By mortal reckoning, it then seems the best way to get to heaven is to be in that laborer group that was hired at the eleventh hour, having to work very little but still gaining the same pay. If the penny were the only blessing, then I'd say that was correct. But there is another blessing that is often overlooked. You see, in the allegorical "day" of our labor, we toil alongside the Savior. When we are engaged in His work, we enjoy His Spirit, His blessing, and His comfort. Those who work for twelve hours get to spend *the entire day* with the Lord, observing Him, learning from Him, and striving to become like Him. Those who only get one hour with the Lord are at a significant deficit compared to the others. When you consider the reward as time spent in the service of God, then twelve hours for a penny seems like the best choice.

How better to get the Savior's image in our countenance than by working alongside Him as much as we can? Indeed, King Benjamin taught, "For how knoweth a man the master whom he has not served, and who is a stranger unto him, and is far from the thoughts and intents of his heart?" (Mosiah 5:13). We achieve the mighty change of heart, deepening our conversion, as we labor in the Lord's work and seek to do His will. When we sacrifice our time to serve others, we change our character to become like His, to the point where we truly have His image as our own. Mormon taught this point eloquently: "Wherefore, my beloved brethren, pray unto the Father with all the energy of heart, that ye may be filled with this love, which he hath bestowed upon all who are true followers of his Son, Jesus Christ; that ye may become the sons of God; *that when he shall appear we shall be like him*, for we shall see him as he is; that we may have this hope; that we may be purified even as he is pure" (Moroni 7:48; emphasis added).

Wouldn't it be amazing if when the Savior appears, we "shall be like Him?" That outcome is completely possible as we seek for the mighty change of heart taught by Alma the Younger. But even as Alma questioned those in Zarahemla whether they had experienced this change of heart, he had an even more important question that we'll review in the next chapter.

Questions for self-reflection:

How much of your testimony is in your mind? How much of it is in your heart? What can you do to deepen your personal conversion to the gospel?

When you consider the future, how much hope do you feel? How much fear do you feel? What can you do to increase hope and decrease fear?

Whose image is in your countenance? What changes do you need to make to better reflect the Savior's life in your own?

CHAPTER FIVE

"Can Ye Feel So Now?"

After having established the importance of spiritual rebirth and some of the behaviors that facilitate this process, Alma the Younger turned to a topic that is more critical on a day-to-day basis. As we've discussed, spiritual rebirth represents a change in direction that helps us return to our Father in Heaven. But just because a person is on the correct path does not mean they'll stay on it. Continuing motivation is necessary. Alma described it this way: "And now behold, I say unto you, my brethren, if ye have experienced a change of heart, and if ye have felt to sing the song of redeeming love, I would ask, can ye feel so now?" (Alma 5:26).

I love the idea of "singing the song of redeeming love." To me this seems like an overwhelming feeling of appreciation and gratitude that is so profound that one cannot help but to erupt in joyous song. It is a far cry from my days of teaching seminary, where the students' early morning singing often resulted in a weak performance. Singing the song of redeeming love is powerful and almost unrestrained. Here are some scriptural examples of this experience:

- D&C 128:22: "Let the earth break forth into singing." Can you imagine the rocks and hills and streams bursting out in song, praising their creator?

- Job 38:7: "When the morning stars sang together, and all the sons of God shouted for joy." When Heavenly Father presented the plan of salvation, do you think someone had to pass out hymnals and invite us to sing? Not remotely! We could scarcely contain ourselves as we sang with all our hearts.

- 3 Nephi 4:31: "And it came to pass that they did break forth, all as one, in singing, and praising their God for the great thing which he had done for them." After being spared from the Gadianton robbers, the Nephites were overwhelmed with gratitude and their thankful souls sang with fervor.

Another one of my favorite examples is from the lives of Alma the Younger and his friend and former partner in crime, Ammon. After their conversion, we know Alma went on to lead the church. Ammon and his colleagues served a fourteen-year mission to the Lamanites and enjoyed great success. While they were on their mission, they crossed paths with Alma. It appears they had not seen each other for many years. This was long before the days of easy communication, so not only had they not seen each other, they probably had little idea of what the others had done. Knowing their respective histories, they likely wondered if the other parties had remained faithful after their conversion. As they met, finding they had all stayed true to the gospel, their joy was overwhelming: "And it came to pass that as Ammon was going forth into the land, that he and his brethren met Alma, over in the place of which has been spoken; and behold, this was a joyful meeting. Now the joy of Ammon was so great even that he was full; yea, he was swallowed up in the joy of his God, even to the exhausting of his strength; and he fell again to the earth. Now was not this exceeding joy? Behold, this is joy which none receiveth save it be the truly penitent and humble seeker of happiness" (Alma 27:16-18).

I love how Ammon was so completely overwhelmed with joy and gratitude that he passed out! Maybe if he hadn't gone unconscious, he would have broken forth into singing. Perhaps you have never spontaneously burst forth into song, but you have probably had experiences where you were amazed at the Lord's mercies and felt incredibly grateful. I previously mentioned how I recently attended a stake conference where Elder Bednar presided. During the general session, Elder Bednar made a last-minute change to the program. We were scheduled to sing *How Firm a Foundation* as the intermediate hymn. He asked that we sing it to close the meeting. Then he said, as close as I can remember, "Brothers and sisters, we are going to sing *How Firm a Foundation*. I would like us to sing all seven verses. This is a song about grace. When you sing it, I want you to think about the lyrics and the wonderful things the Savior has done for you."

I don't think I had ever sung that entire hymn before. I was familiar with the amazing seventh verse as the Tabernacle Choir at Temple Square performs a beautiful arrangement of the hymn that includes that verse. But I hadn't thought about the other verses as much. I chose to accept Elder Bednar's invitation and thought about the Savior's grace as I sang the hymn. I was completely overwhelmed. I wept throughout the singing, sometimes uncontrollably. When you get a minute, go and look at the lyrics. The first six verses build upon each other, talking about how the Lord will never abandon us despite trials and difficulties. Then comes verse seven, where we affirm our commitment to Him:

> *The soul that on Jesus hath leaned for repose*
> *I will not, I cannot, desert to his foes;*
> *That soul, thou all hell should endeavor to shake,*
> *I'll never, no never, I'll never, no never,*
> *I'll never, no never, no never forsake!* [5]

Even typing these lyrics thrills my soul. As I sang the words, invited to do so by an apostle of Jesus Christ, I felt a deep level of

---

5 *Hymns of The Church of Jesus Christ of Latter-day Saints* (Salt Lake City: The Church of Jesus Christ of Latter-day Saints, 1985) no. 85.

commitment. How could I reject the One who had been with me all the time? I couldn't, I wouldn't, and my heart sang forth with a promise that I would truly never forsake.

When Alma talks about "singing the song of redeeming love," I believe this is the type of joy and amazement that he refers to. It is Ammon's meeting with Alma, the Nephites praising God for their deliverance, and my intense gratitude for a Savior who will never abandon me. Then comes the question that is relevant for all of us: "if ye have felt to sing the song of redeeming love, I would ask, *can ye feel so now?*" (Alma 5:26; emphasis added). After the deliverance, the joyous reunions, or the amazing hymns with apostles, what happens then? Do we continue with our firm resolve or do we fall back into old habits? This question is critical for all on the covenant path.

C.S. Lewis, the master Christian apologist, wrote a remarkable book called *The Screwtape Letters.* It is a collection of correspondences from an experienced devil, Screwtape, to his nephew and apprentice devil, Wormwood. Wormwood has been given a man to tempt as his first assignment. He writes to his Uncle Screwtape with questions and concerns. Screwtape responds with sage advice about how to effectively keep this man from the paths of righteousness. At one point, Wormwood reveals that his charge has begun attending church. Screwtape admonishes Wormwood for being so careless to let the man find a church in the first place: "I note with grave displeasure that your patient has become a Christian.... In the meantime we must make the best of the situation. There is no need to despair; hundreds of these adult converts have been reclaimed after a brief sojourn in the Enemy's camp and are now with us. All the habits of the patient, both mental and bodily, are still in our favor." [6]

Screwtape goes on to advise Wormwood on next steps. He encourages him to help his patient focus on the flaws of his

---

6   C.S. Lewis, *The Screwtape Letters* (New York: HarperCollins, 2001) 5.

church associates, such as strange clothing, idiosyncratic behaviors, or even out-of-tune singing. Screwtape promises that as long as the individual can keep his focus off the gospel and on the more annoying and distracting things, he will eventually leave the faith and return to his former paths. With the exception of scripture, I'm not sure truer words have ever been written. If the devil has a playbook, which I believe he does, this strategy is chapter and verse from his evil handbook of instruction. In his efforts to help us forget those incredible moments where we sang the song of redeeming love, Satan uses two primary tactics. First, he wants us to disbelieve in truth. If he can't accomplish that, then he will try to distract us to the point where our beliefs make little difference anyway. Let's talk about these strategies.

I believe the genius of the Church of Jesus Christ of Latter-day Saints is that all individuals, whether current members or those considering membership, can receive a personal witness of the truth of the restored gospel. This witness comes from God, not man. The Savior taught this when Peter bore testimony of Jesus' divinity. As the Lord inquired about who the disciples believed Him to be, Peter witnessed that Jesus was the Christ. The Lord responded, "Blessed art thou, Simon Bar-jona: for flesh and blood hath not revealed it unto thee, but my Father which is in heaven" (Matthew 16:17). In other words, the Savior said, "Simon, you are blessed because your knowledge that I am the Christ did not come from man, or an earthly study of things, but came from my Father through the witness of the Holy Ghost." Each of us can receive a similar witness of any aspect of truth, whether it be the reality of a Savior, the veracity of the Book of Mormon, or the importance of keeping commandments.

However, once we have received such a witness, we must continue to nurture our testimony in order for it to stay strong. You could very accurately compare it to a plant. When you grow a plant from a seed, you must take great care to ensure the seed will sprout. Good soil, water, fertilizer, and sunlight are all necessary.

Once the plant is grown and the roots are strong, it needs ongoing nourishment. If it fails to receive nourishment for an extended period of time, the plant will die, regardless of how deep the roots or how robust the foliage. Like plants, testimonies die if not properly nourished.

Many years ago, I read a blog post from a disaffected member of the Church of Jesus Christ of Latter-day Saints. This person remarked how he had grown up in the church, served a full-time mission, been a bishop, but had since fallen away. In his remarks, he noted how he didn't believe the church was true, doubted the authenticity of the Book of Mormon, and was convinced Joseph Smith was a fraud. I remember thinking, "This guy is a liar! There's no way he could have served a mission, where he testified of gospel truths *every day*, and now claim he doesn't believe they are true." I figured he *still* believed but for whatever reason felt compelled to declare to the contrary. Since then, I've come to realize that person probably wasn't a liar at all. In fact, I believe he was being quite sincere. I think he truly lost his faith in restored gospel truths.

I used to believe that a testimony of truth, the kind you get from the Holy Ghost, was like a treasure chest. Once you received it, you could display it prominently in your home. If you neglected it, it might get dusty or tarnished, but a quick rub with a clean cloth would make it shine once more. I was very wrong. Like we discussed previously, testimony is like a plant. It is a living, breathing thing. It will not survive long periods of neglect. On the other hand, it will increase in strength and size if properly cared for. Satan wants us to lose our testimony of truth. He wants our "testimony plant" to be brown, dead, and cast into the garbage. For those who have "sung the song of redeeming love," he wants them to forget the lyrics, forget the tune, and lose the songbook altogether. In some cases, he succeeds, and such individuals abandon their faith. However, I believe this approach is less successful than some of Lucifer's more subtle and sophisticated plans.

Many people have strengthened their testimonies for a very long time. They won't discard something they've worked so hard to obtain. Usually they realize the value of what they have and remember the time and effort it took to develop. Satan knows the efforts made by most church members to obtain a testimony. He knows they are unlikely to just cast it aside. Instead, he encourages chronic *but not severe* neglect. In the plant analogy, he wants us to keep the plant alive, but barely. Here are a few examples of this strategy:

> "And there shall also be many which shall say: Eat, drink, and be merry; nevertheless, fear God—*he will justify in committing a little sin*; yea, lie a little, take the advantage of one because of his words, dig a pit for thy neighbor; there is no harm in this; and do all these things, for tomorrow we die; and if it so be that we are guilty, God will beat us with a few stripes, and at last we shall be saved in the kingdom of God." (2 Nephi 28:8, emphasis added)

> "And others will he pacify, and lull them away into carnal security, that they will say: All is well in Zion; yea, Zion prospereth, all is well—and thus the devil cheateth their souls, and *leadeth them away carefully down to hell*." (2 Nephi 28:21, emphasis added)

> "And behold, others he flattereth away, and telleth them there is no hell; and he saith unto them: I am no devil, for there is none—*and thus he whispereth in their ears*, until he grasps them with his awful chains, from whence there is no deliverance." (2 Nephi 28:22, emphasis added)

These temptation strategies are brilliant and highly effective. If I weren't so frustrated with the chaos Satan constantly stirs up in my life and the lives of those I love, I'd feel inclined to shake his hand for being so expertly crafty. Note the patience and careful execution as he "leads carefully" and "whispers" his lies and half-truths. He rightly speaks of the mercies of God, but then falsely claims such mercies will be used to excuse our accountability for sinful behavior. As this applies to our plant of testimony, Satan would say, "That's a very lovely plant. You worked hard to grow it and should be proud of your efforts. The last thing I'd want is for you to throw that plant away. But does it really need to be watered every day? I mean, look how green the leaves are! And those roots must be at least a foot deep! Sure, you should tend to it when you can, but you can probably get away with taking a break at times; the plant will survive. Don't you deserve a break? I sure think you do."

Of course, he is lying. He wants nothing more than for your testimony plant to die and be cast out forever. But he is willing to wait years and even decades for that to happen, as long as he eventually gets his way. He wants our testimonies to be half-dead, barely serving their purpose, *but still alive*. If we were to compare this to singing the song of redeeming love, this would be where we still have the songbook, but it is dusty and hard to locate. We can partially recall the tune, but it is a distant memory. There are days when we can't even remember the song at all. Yet we feel good about still having the songbook and having sung the song before. Even then, the once powerful effect of that marvelous melody has long since lost its influence in our lives.

If that weren't enough, I believe Satan has *yet another* strategy to disrupt our testimonies. For some, when he presents his "Don't you deserve a break?" temptation, they respond, "No! I know that my plant needs daily care. I am fully committed to the upkeep and nurture of this plant and will not abandon my efforts." Following your rebuke, if you think Lucifer walks away with his head hung low, acknowledging defeat, think again. He's got one more trick up his sleeve to get that plant to wither and that tune to fade from your memory. This game plan is titled "distraction." In this plan, Satan doesn't even try to argue our point that the plant needs nourishment. "You're right," he states. "Your plant needs daily care. But don't forget about the other important things in life. You need to exercise, develop your talents, enrich your career, take time for self-care, check things off your bucket list, etc..."

This may be the most effective strategy of all, because the adversary is able to get us to choose so many other activities that we simply don't have time to care for our testimonies. He convinces us that we are engaged in worthy and responsible tasks. Sometimes this is quite easy, because our busyness *often* consists of worthy and responsible tasks. There is nothing wrong with increasing education, taking care of personal needs, traveling, improving health, or a thousand other wonderful things. But if these tasks come at the expense of caring for faith and testimony, then we've made a poor decision. Time is a limited quantity, and when we spend time doing one thing it necessarily means that we cannot spend that same portion of time doing something else. President Dallin H. Oaks stated the following: "We make many choices between two goods, often involving how we will spend our time. There is nothing bad about playing video games or texting or watching TV or talking on a cell phone. But each of these involves what is called "opportunity cost," meaning that if we spend time doing one thing, we lose the opportunity to do another. I am sure you can see that we need to measure thoughtfully what we are losing by the time we spend on one activity, even if it is perfectly good in itself." [7]

Modern society is filled with distractions, perhaps as never before. There are constant demands for our time. Some of these demands are worthier than others. Simply wanting to keep your plant alive does not work if you do not invest the effort to nurture it. I believe Satan is just as content with an overscheduled, spiritually weakening member whose testimony is dying from neglect as he is with a disaffected former member of the church. To return to the song of redeeming love analogy, the "distracted" circumstance

---

7   Dallin H. Oaks, "Where Will This Lead?" *Ensign*, May 2019, 61.

is when we still have the songbook, we fondly remember the times we have sung, but we are just too busy to sing. We cannot allow the good things in life to get in the way of things that are essential to our spiritual development.

Alma the Younger had truly sung the song of redeeming love. I imagine that he also had some experience with occasionally feeling distant from the Spirit, as is the case with all mortals. He knew the importance of rekindling testimony when it starts to fade. We are all in similar situations. There are times when our fire of faith is blazing and intense. Other times that same fire can get down to a flicker. This is common to the human condition and is nothing to be ashamed of. However, we have an obligation to stoke the flames when they die down. Alma knew that many of his contemporary saints were spiritually frail. Their plants of testimony were dying. It had been years since they had sung the song of redeeming love. In true prophetic fashion, he had a plan for their recovery. His plan can be used for any of us who want to have longer periods of spiritual strength and fewer episodes of spiritual weakness. The following chapters detail Alma's specific strategies to help us obtain such strength.

Questions for self-reflection:

When have you felt to "sing the song of redeeming love"? What keeps you from feeling that now?

Examine the current status of your testimony of the gospel of Jesus Christ. How healthy is it? Does it need more nourishment? What can you do to strengthen your testimony of truth?

Consider Satan's strategies of neglect, apathy and distraction. To what degree is your testimony affected by these? What changes can you make to better prevent against such temptations?

CHAPTER SIX

"Have Ye Walked, Keeping Yourself Blameless Before God?"

Immediately following his question "can ye feel so now," Alma the Younger asked his audience: "Have ye walked, keeping yourselves blameless before God?.... That your garments have been cleansed and made white through the blood of Christ, who will come to redeem his people from their sins?" (Alma 5:27).

This seems like a very difficult task. Do any of you feel blameless before God? Do you believe your lives are free from the stain of sin, having been fully purified through the blood of Christ? If you do feel this way, I'm very impressed and you can probably stop reading. But I believe that almost everyone has ongoing feelings of blame and continual awareness of their sins and shortcomings. When I hear our modern prophets and apostles talk about their own need for repentance and improvement, it often feels like this concept of being "blameless" might be unattainable. But as members of the restored church of Jesus Christ, there is more to this concept than we often consider.

Often, we view the idea of being blameless and free from sin as occurring in a very future day. We see ourselves standing before God to be judged. We know the blood of the Lamb will be sufficient to purify any remaining stain. Through our faithful efforts during life, in that moment we can qualify for mercy, and our residual imperfections will be removed once and for all. Yet Alma the Younger seems to refer to an *ongoing and current* process, something happening in real time for diligent disciples of Christ. To better appreciate this principle, we need to understand the difference between "obtaining a remission of sins" and "retaining a remission of sins."

We "obtain" a remission of sins through the saving ordinances of the gospel of Jesus Christ. As I mentioned at the beginning of this book, I remember being baptized at eight years of age and having a feeling of purity like never before. As we are baptized and confirmed by proper authority, we obtain a remission of sins. Many who receive this ordinance describe a feeling of cleanliness and renewal. But that feeling doesn't last, as we are constantly challenged with temptations and eventually yield to sin. I remember thinking that it would be great to be baptized again, so I could have that same feeling of freshness. Even though that is not the Lord's plan, He has made arrangements so we can feel spiritually clean on a regular basis. Elder David A. Bednar taught as follows:

> Sometimes Latter-day Saints express the wish that they could be baptized again—and thereby become as clean and worthy as the day on which they received their first saving gospel ordinance. May I respectfully suggest that our Heavenly Father and His Beloved Son do not intend for us to experience such a feeling of spiritual renewal, refreshment, and restoration just once in our lives. The blessings of obtaining and always retaining a remission of our sins through gospel ordinances help us understand that baptism is a point of departure in our mortal spiritual journey; it is not a destination we should yearn to revisit over and over again. [8]

---

8   David A. Bednar, "Always Retain a Remission of Your Sins." *Ensign*, May 2016, 62.

Those initial ordinances of baptism and confirmation are the beginning of the path. They provide great joy. As we continue our journey, we find additional opportunities to feel forgiveness, happiness, and powerful gratitude so great that we burst into the song of redeeming love. These opportunities don't come on their own; we must act and prepare for them.

I have always believed that the language of scripture is very intentional, down to the last word. I think of Mormon creating the golden plates and then trying to summarize one thousand years of history into a single, portable volume. I think of Moroni being worried about his poor dexterity when writing on plates and how future generations might mock his words (see Ether 12:25-26). Surely, they gave careful consideration to each word. As I read the scriptures, I try to notice specific phrases and what implication they have. The following scripture has great meaning to me.

As Alma the Younger talks about daily diligence to remain on the path, he says, "*Have ye walked*, keeping yourselves blameless before God?" (Alma 5:27, emphasis added). Maybe it's just the psychologist in me, but I think there is meaning in the phrase "have ye walked." Note what the scripture *doesn't* say. It doesn't say, "have ye sat," or "have ye wandered," or "have ye had someone carry you." It says "have ye walked." Can you see how this implies a righteous exercise of agency? There is intentionality and purpose in the statement. It presumes action and direction on our part.

Many years ago, one of our sons was a member of the Boy Scouts of America. He wanted to earn his hiking merit badge, which among other things, required a twenty-mile hike. My family and I are not really campers or outdoorsy people. I love nature but typically prefer to admire from a safe distance. When my son asked if I could take him on a twenty-mile hike, I readily agreed and then immediately wondered how to do this, considering 1) I was unfamiliar with the local trails and 2) it would take about a million loops around our backyard to reach that distance. As I researched the requirements, I read that an "urban hike" would suffice. It was music to my ears. All we had to do was walk twenty miles in town, on paved sidewalks, with GPS navigation to assist. This was going to be easy.

We prepared and outlined our route. Our son invited a friend who truly had no idea what he was getting into. My wife had a meeting that evening so we needed to return in time to care for the younger children. No problem, I thought. We would start early and return early. I mapped out a course that would take us to a favorite fast food restaurant that was ten miles away. We'd go there, have lunch, and then come home. As we started the hike, our pace was brisk, and we all felt great. Minutes turned into hours and we still felt pretty good. My son and his friend were joking with each other, climbing on small ledges, and doing acrobatic tricks along the way. We stopped at a grocery store to get "supplies." The kids bought candy and soda; I was more responsible and bought something that looked nutritious, but I intentionally avoided reading the ingredients. As we reached seven miles, I remember thinking, "This is a pretty long hike." I don't think I'd ever walked that far in one day. The boys started to fatigue, but their spirits were still high. Eventually we reached the half-way mark, fueled up on greasy hamburgers and French fries, and headed home.

The return journey was pretty miserable. I had severely underestimated the toll of hard pavement on my feet after five hours of walking. The boys took more frequent breaks. Under normal circumstances this would have been fine, but we needed to be home by a certain time. I gently encouraged them to take short breaks despite my own desire to collapse. In addition, the sun glared down and our misery grew by the minute. We stopped at a grocery store to use the bathroom. The air-conditioning felt wonderful. Both boys literally spread out on the bathroom floor on the cool tile. If we weren't so exhausted, we probably would have thought that was pretty disgusting. We resumed our journey and plodded down the path that we had skipped along just hours earlier. I remember the boys sitting down just one mile from home. The look on their faces said, "We can't go another step." I did my best to rally them and keep going, especially as our time to reach home was running short. Eventually we made it home and collapsed in the front yard. My legs and feet were sore for an entire week.

The requirement was to take a twenty-mile hike in a single day. We couldn't have done it on a bicycle. We couldn't have divided the journey into forty half-mile walks. We couldn't have someone push us in a giant stroller. We had to do it on our own. It was difficult and even miserable at times, but in order to earn that particular scouting award, we had to do it for ourselves. When Alma the Younger says "Have ye walked, keeping yourself blameless before God," I think it means we are responsible for our own spiritual progression. We cannot assign our progression to others or make excuses for our lack of movement. Sitting down gets us nowhere. Wandering makes us feel like we are doing something, but there is no progression. Having someone carry us completely defeats the purpose of spiritual growth. Action is always required for personal progress, and action begins with awareness that we alone are accountable for our spiritual development. Personal responsibility is the first step in keeping ourselves blameless before God.

Baptism and confirmation are how we "obtain" a remission of sins. Then what of the continuing process of "retaining" a remission of sins? Elder Bednar further taught, "As members of the Lord's restored Church, we are blessed both by our *initial cleansing from sin* associated with baptism and by the potential for an *ongoing cleansing from sin* made possible through the companionship and power of the Holy Ghost—even the third member of the Godhead." [9] The companionship of the Holy Ghost is the purifying and sanctifying influence that provides ongoing remission of sins. As we allow the Spirit to be our constant companion, we become less and less like the natural man or woman and more and more like the man or

---

9   David A. Bednar, "Always Retain a Remission of Your Sins." *Ensign*, May 2016, 61.

woman of Christ. Obviously, there are many, many things we can do to increase the presence of the Holy Spirit in our lives, such as prayer, scripture study, worthy partaking of the sacrament, temple attendance, and much more. However, both Mormon and King Benjamin provide additional insight into one very specific thing we can do to *retain* a remission of our sins.

In Alma chapter 4, Mormon comments on the wicked state of the church in Zarahemla. He notes how most members of the church were off the covenant path, but a smaller group had remained faithful. Mormon points out how the disobedient members had become haughty, withholding assistance from the poor. The righteous continued to share their meager means with the needy. Mormon described the actions of the obedient saints as follows: "[They succored] those who stood in need of their succor, such as imparting their substance to the poor and the needy, feeding the hungry, and suffering all manner of afflictions, for Christ's sake, who should come according to the spirit of prophecy; Looking forward to that day, *thus retaining a remission of their sins*" (Alma 4:13-14, emphasis added). As they cared for the poor and needy, they *retained* a remission of their sins. They increased in spiritual strength and purity and became more like the Savior.

About forty years prior, King Benjamin gave remarkable counsel to his faithful subjects. He talked specifically about providing for the poor and needy, addressing questions about charitable contributions that still arise today. "And now, for the sake of these things which I have spoken unto you—that is, *for the sake of retaining a remission of your sins from day to day, that ye may walk guiltless before God*—I would that ye should impart of your substance to the poor, every man according to that which he hath, such as feeding the hungry, clothing the naked, visiting the sick and administering to their relief, both spiritually and temporally, according to their wants" (Mosiah 4:26; emphasis added). This is the same principle that Mormon taught. Caring for the poor and needy leads to an ongoing remission of sins and spiritual sanctification.

As far as I can tell, those are the only scriptures that use the specific words "retaining a remission of sins," and they *all* talk about helping the poor and needy. I'm not exactly certain why this is the case, but I have some theories as to how caring for the poor connects to retaining a remission of sins. The ongoing process of purification from sin helps us become like Jesus Christ. Among the Savior's amazing characteristics, perhaps one of the grandest is the way He cares for others. His whole life was about helping the less fortunate. He specifically helped the downtrodden and outcasts. His teachings and parables showed His concern for those who were rejected by others. There is one account from the Savior's life that I particularly love. I believe it clearly demonstrates His compassion for others.

In the 19th chapter of Luke, the Savior passes through the town of Jericho. By then His fame was widespread and many gathered to see Him. Zacchaeus was a publican, or tax collector. Those of his profession had the reputation of being dishonest thieves. As such, they were poorly regarded by the Jewish community. Yet Zacchaeus was a righteous man who believed in Jesus Christ. He wanted to see Him as he passed through his town. Unfortunately for him, he was short and could not see Jesus through the large crowd that had gathered. Not letting his small stature stop him, he climbed a tree in order to catch a glimpse of the Son of God.

Surely Jesus had many important things to do every day. His mortal ministry was only three years. In that period, He had to establish a church, teach doctrine, and prepare his apostles to lead the kingdom without Him. But He was always eager and took the time to bless people one by one. As He passed through the large crowd, Jesus saw Zacchaeus in the tree. "And when Jesus came to the place, he looked up, and saw him, and said unto him, Zacchaeus, make haste, and come down; for today I must abide at thy house. And he made haste, and came down, and received him joyfully" (Luke 19:5-6). Imagine the thrill for Zacchaeus! This short fellow had only hoped to catch a peek of the Savior and

55

now the Lord would be a guest at his house. Surely this was the highlight of a lifetime.

I love the Lord's response: "For today I *must* abide at thy house." Certainly, the Savior did not *need* to stay with Zacchaeus. He likely had many offers and options of lodging for the evening. But He chose this faithful man, who was wrongfully despised by so many, to have a one-on-one teaching and ministering experience. This is the way the Savior operates. He helps those who need it most. He seeks out the weak and lowly. He rescues those who have no hope of making it on their own. Whether seeking after lost sheep or spotting earnest believers in trees, His pattern is to help those who are less fortunate. Perhaps as we love and care for our fellow men, we also develop this most desirable Messianic characteristic of charity and love.

The Savior has commanded us to care for the poor and needy. Caring for these individuals can be difficult, especially when dealing with those who appear to have created their own miserable situation. There are times when I have felt to withhold support for fear that I would simply enable someone's negative lifestyle. Have you ever known someone in need, but felt like they caused their own grief? For example, what about the poorly educated who cannot find decent employment? Or the chronic spender who cannot rent an apartment due to several bankruptcies? When you are presented with the opportunity to help such individuals, have you thought something like this? "How is he going to learn to improve his life if I just bail him out? I shouldn't give him anything. He needs to experience the consequence of his poor choices." I am well familiar with that such thinking because I have often considered it. Is this line of thought justified? I'm not sure it is.

Evidently this reasoning has been present for a very long time, as King Benjamin specifically addressed it decades before the coming of Christ: "And also, ye yourselves will succor those that stand in need of your succor; ye will administer of your substance unto him that standeth in need; and ye will not suffer that the beggar putteth up his petition to you in vain, and turn him out to perish" (Mosiah 4:16). In other words, we should give to the poor and needy, as the Spirit directs, even to those who have caused their own problems. But what about our fears or enabling irresponsible behavior? King Benjamin answered that as well. "Perhaps thou shalt say: The man has brought upon himself his misery; therefore I will stay my hand, and will not give unto him of my food, nor impart unto him of my substance that he may not suffer, for his punishments are just— But I say unto you, O man, whosoever doeth this the same hath great cause to repent; and except he repenteth of that which he hath done he perisheth forever, and hath no interest in the kingdom of God" (Mosiah 4:17). The caution is pretty clear; we should be as generous as possible and follow the Spirit's direction to help others.

King Benjamin's most compelling argument comes next. "For behold, are we not all beggars? Do we not all depend upon the same Being, even God, for all the substance which we have, for both food and raiment, and for gold, and for silver, and for all the riches which we have of every kind?" (Mosiah 4:18). Can anyone even begin to argue with this amazing doctrine? King Benjamin is absolutely correct. Regardless of our standing, we are all desperately dependent upon our Father in Heaven for *everything* we have, down to each breath we take. How can I look down my nose at a less fortunate person when I realize that the very fact I even *have* a nose is because of a generous, majestic Heavenly Father?

This is not a sermon or recommendation regarding *how* you should support those in need. It *is* a sermon regarding how becoming more like Christ and retaining a remission of sins depends on being generous with our time and means and seeking to bless the lives of others at every turn. This is a very practical step that everyone can take in order to keep themselves blameless before God, per Alma's counsel (see Alma 5:27). Surely there are many ways to retain a remission of sins, and this is one that can be universally practiced. Even those who don't have enough money for themselves can provide emotional support to those who suffer. There is always something we can do to bless the lives of those around us.

Developing greater spiritual strength includes being accountable for our own spiritual progression. We must strive to keep our covenants on a daily basis. In addition, as we practice principles of charity and giving to those in need, we can keep our spiritual flames burning bright while minimizing times of spiritual apathy.

Questions for self-reflection:

Do you feel responsible for your own spiritual progression? What are some things you can do to become even more cleansed from sin?

Consider a time in your life when the Lord has answered your prayers. How can remembering this experience help you be more compassionate towards others?

What can you do to increase acts of charity towards others?

CHAPTER SEVEN

"Have Ye Been Sufficiently Humble?"

Alma the Younger continues to address the people of Zarahemla, providing thought-provoking questions that resonate with us today. In his desire to help them maintain spiritual strength through challenges, he asks: "Could ye say, if ye were called to die at this time, within yourselves, that ye have been sufficiently humble?" (Alma 5:27). Humility is a key characteristic that brings us closer to God.

One would think humility might come naturally to humans. When I was a full-time missionary in Mexico we often lived in rural locations. I remember going to teach a family that lived in a remote area. I had only been in Mexico for a few days and everything was quite new to me. My companion and I arrived at the small town late in the day. We hiked down a ravine to the shacks where the family lived. It was very, very dark as I looked up at the clear night sky. The stars were incredible; I don't think I've ever seen so many of them. It was beautiful and overwhelming at the same time. I felt pretty small when I considered my relative size and place in the universe.

Prophets have had visions that helped them see things in an eternal context. Enoch related the following: "And were it possible that man could number the particles of the earth, yea, millions of earths like this, it would not be a beginning to the number of thy creations; and thy curtains are stretched out still" (Moses 7:30). Although it seems fantastic, this is not an exaggeration. Enoch is saying if you could count each particle, or perhaps each atom, in this world, and millions of other worlds like this, that number would not even *begin* to describe the number of Father's creations. To provide context, there are approximately seven billion billion billion atoms in your body. That's a seven with 27 zeros after it. And that's just in *your* body. The number of particles in the *entire world* is astronomical. Based on Enoch's statement, we can imagine the incredibly massive number of God's creations and our relatively small place in it all.

Moses had a similar experience that helped him gain humility. Although he was a Hebrew, he grew up among Egyptian royalty. Egyptians considered pharaohs to be gods, and Moses probably believed this as well. After his call to be a prophet, Moses had an experience where he was visited by the true God. "And [Moses] saw God face to face, and he talked with him, and the glory of God was upon Moses; therefore Moses could endure his presence" (Moses 1:2). Note how Moses' mortal body had to be transfigured such that he could withstand the awesome presence of God without being consumed. After the heavenly visit, the transfiguring power departed from him. "And the presence of God withdrew from Moses, that his glory was not upon Moses; and Moses was left unto himself. And as he was left unto himself, he fell unto the earth" (Moses 1:9). The scriptures comment that Moses was physically exhausted after the visit and it took many hours to regain his strength. Moses remarks: "Now, for *this cause I know that man is nothing, which thing I never had supposed*. But now mine own eyes have beheld God; but not my natural, but my spiritual eyes, for my natural eyes could not have beheld; for I should have withered and died in his presence; but his glory was upon me; and I beheld his face, for I was transfigured before him" (Moses 1:10-11, emphasis added). After experiencing the glory of the true God compared to the "glory" of Egyptian pharaohs, Moses truly knew that man was insignificant compared to heavenly beings.

Based on our miniscule position in the universe and our puny power when compared to God, one might presume that mankind would be naturally humble. Yet the opposite is true. Our base natures tend to be proud, as we often seek to exalt ourselves over others. Paul taught the Romans, "the carnal mind is enmity against God" (Romans 8:7). Enmity means to be in active opposition towards something or someone. Frankly, it is an apt description of Satan. He has been actively opposed to God ever since his first rebellion.

I have often reflected on Lucifer's boldness as he presented his devious plan in the grand councils of heaven. The plan of salvation was designed by our Father in Heaven. It was perfect. Even though it carried the risk of not everyone returning to God's presence, it ensured that all who truly desired to return would be able to. In my mind's eye I see us standing in awe as the plan is revealed and shouting for joy at our newfound heavenly potential. As the meeting draws to a close, Lucifer stands up. I'm pretty sure he was not on the agenda. He presents his diabolical scheme that would strip us of agency, even though agency was critical to Father's plan. "Behold, here am I, send me, I will be thy son, and I will redeem all mankind, that one soul shall not be lost, and surely I will do it" (Moses 4:1). Then he adds the devilish caveat, bringing his thinly veiled motivation into focus: "wherefore give me thine honor" (Moses 4:1). Note how there are only 35 words in Satan's statement and yet he refers to himself *six times*. It is no wonder the natural man, who commonly follows Satan's influence, typically lacks humility.

Alma the Younger asked the Zarahemla saints if they had been sufficiently humble. Then he posed another interesting question. "Behold, are ye stripped of pride?" (Alma 5:28) Why would he ask if they had removed pride from their lives after asking them to be humble? If they had eliminated pride, doesn't that presume the presence of humility? I don't believe it does. I think becoming truly humble requires two separate steps. First, we must eliminate pride. Second, we must develop Christlike humility. Let's talk about these two steps.

In President Ezra Taft Benson's seminal general conference address entitled "Beware of Pride," he defined pride as follows: "The central feature of pride is enmity—enmity toward God and enmity toward our fellowmen.... Our enmity toward God takes on many labels, such as rebellion, hard-heartedness, stiff-neckedness, unrepentant, puffed up, easily offended, and sign seekers. The proud wish God would agree with them. They aren't interested in changing their opinions to agree with God's." [10] Pride is so short-sighted! President Benson's comment that "the proud wish God would agree with them" is quite descriptive of our current society. It reminds me of a personal experience that highlighted my own tendency towards pride.

We recently had a mysterious water leak in our home. After discovering the problem, we searched through the home and couldn't find the source of the leak. Ultimately, we called a plumber. I had never met this person before. He came out to the house, did a few quick tests, and concluded that our main water line was leaking. He recommended replacement at a cost of $2,500. Notwithstanding the significant cost and the fact that I could not independently verify his conclusion, *I didn't doubt him for a second*. I simply accepted his recommendation and arranged for the repair.

In contrast, on occasion I will receive a prompting from the Holy Ghost. Often, such promptings will be contrary to my plans. I'm ashamed to say that far too frequently, my first reaction is to question the prompting and search for a different solution. Evidently I'm willing to immediately accept the expensive

---

10 Ezra Taft Benson, "Beware of Pride." *Ensign,* May 1989, https://www.lds.org/general-conference/1989/04/beware-of-pride?lang=eng.

recommendation of an unknown plumber, but I doubt the promptings of the Almighty God? Does that seem a little strange to you as well? I suppose when put into that perspective, it seems completely foolish to question the Spirit, but for many it is a very natural reaction. Perhaps we all need to learn how to agree with God as readily as we often agree with mortal "experts."

One of the main things we can do to eliminate pride is to truly understand our position before God. Pride wants us to challenge God, pitting our desires against His. The absence of pride helps us accept His will. I am reminded of the New Testament account when Jesus was arrested. He had just finished his experience in the garden of Gethsemane, which was excruciating to say the least. As He anticipated the upcoming torture of Calvary, a group of armed men approached. These were temple guards who served as "law enforcement" to bring Jesus in for questioning. They were led by the traitor, Judas Iscariot. Jesus asked them a simple question. Their reaction was noteworthy: "Jesus therefore, knowing all things that should come upon him, went forth, and said unto them, Whom seek ye? They answered him, Jesus of Nazareth. Jesus saith unto them, I am he. And Judas also, which betrayed him, stood with them. *As soon then as he had said unto them, I am he, they went backward, and fell to the ground*" (Luke 18:4-6, emphasis added).

I find it fascinating that when Jesus announced Himself, at their request, they retreated and fell down. Doesn't that seem a little ironic? These men, who had a job to do, approached the Savior armed and determined. This peacekeeping, unarmed man calmly answered their question and it caused them to collapse. I believe that Jesus' answer to their question was so spiritually powerful that they could not help but fall to the ground. Simply answering "I am he" was practically a declaration of His holy nature. Although these men came to arrest Him, they were overwhelmed by His presence and could scarcely complete the job. This is a stark reminder of how mankind is nothing when compared to God.

Pride before God is based on an inaccurate understanding of His divine nature. Compared to His majesty and power, we are truly nothing. King Benjamin helped illustrate this concept with amazing accuracy: "And now, in the first place, he hath created you, and granted unto you your lives, for which ye are indebted unto him.... And now I ask, can ye say aught of yourselves? I answer you, Nay. Ye cannot say that ye are even as much as the dust of the earth; yet ye were created of the dust of the earth; but behold, it belongeth to him who created you" (Mosiah 2:23, 25). In other words, we wouldn't even exist if it wasn't for Him creating us. Now that we do exist, we are less than the dust beneath our feet. Even if we tried to argue that we were equal to the dust, the dust still wins, because at least it is always obedient to God.

Becoming "stripped of pride" is an active process. If we find it difficult to eliminate this characteristic, perhaps we could embark on a serious study of the nature of Heavenly Father and Jesus Christ. As we rediscover their might and splendor, this can help us put our own lives into proper perspective and be less inclined to reject their counsel.

The second part of this process is to increase humility. As previously noted, I don't think that eliminating pride necessarily promotes humility. I have known many people whose circumstances have reduced them to almost nothing, yet they continue to be angry and proud. Mormon had this experience with his Nephite armies. Towards the end of the Nephite civilization, they engaged in many wars. The Nephites had long since abandoned their righteous ways and were steeped in sin. After a particularly intense battle, the Nephites suffered serious losses. Mormon sensed sadness and dejection in his armies. For a moment his heart took courage, for he knew that defeat and loss can lead to humility and repentance. But he was disappointed as they did not humble themselves but "curse[d] God and wish[ed] to die" (see Mormon 2:12-14). The absence of pride does not always lead to the presence of humility.

If we can eliminate pride from our lives, we also need to actively cultivate humility. However, Satan has clever traps in this area as well. If he sees us abandon pride and try to increase humility, he shifts his focus. He says, "You are correct; you shouldn't be proud. Just look at yourself. There's nothing to be proud of. In fact, you are nothing. You are as worthless as they come. Didn't you just read a scripture about being less than the dust of the earth? Boy, that sounds about right." It is important to realize that humility has nothing to do with feeling worthless. On the contrary, we have infinite value and potential. Elder Dieter F. Uchtdorf of the Quorum of the Twelve Apostles stated: "Some suppose that humility is about beating ourselves up. Humility does not mean convincing ourselves that we are worthless, meaningless, or of little value. Nor does it mean denying or withholding the talents God has given us. We don't discover humility by thinking less *of* ourselves; we discover humility by thinking less *about* ourselves. It comes as we go about our work with an attitude of serving God and our fellowman." [11]

What can we do to increase humility? I have three suggestions:

Pray for humility. I know what many of you might say. "That's dangerous, Brother Morgan. If you pray for humility you are likely to get your socks knocked off through trials." That's probably true. In fact, I've experienced it in my own life. I remember a time when I felt the need to develop greater humility and compassion, so I earnestly prayed and asked for this. About a week later I sustained a debilitating back injury. There were days I couldn't walk without the assistance of a cane. For two months I was in constant pain. Following intense physical therapy and ongoing recuperation, I returned to normal functioning. I understand my experience was very short-lived compared to many others whose chronic illness persists for years and decades. Even so, it taught me an important lesson and I developed greater compassion for others. Although I don't wish to repeat such an experience, I believe the price was

---

11 Dieter F. Uchtdorf, "Pride and the Priesthood." *Ensign*, November 2010, 58.

well worth the resulting blessing. The Lord knows the best ways to teach us. He will help us learn if we ask Him.

Be faithful to covenants. One key to greater humility is being obedient to God's commands. It is very difficult to be disobedient and humble at the same time. For many of us, we have made sacred covenants through baptism and confirmation, being ordained to the holy priesthood, receiving our temple endowment, or being sealed for time and all eternity. Each of these covenants provides an opportunity to submit our will to God. If you are like me, you experience temptation on a daily basis. Such temptations entice us to violate covenants, either through commission or omission. However, resisting temptation and remaining true to covenant promises can result in greater humility.

Commit to follow spiritual promptings. It is one thing to be obedient to our covenants. We typically know what to do to keep on the straight and narrow path. But what about additional spiritual promptings that invite action? Have you ever felt impressed to do something but then wondered if you should follow through? Such promptings are often above and beyond the standard "checklist" of covenant keeping. Sometimes people question whether such impressions are their own thoughts or the Spirit of the Lord. This is a subtle art and usually takes much practice and increased spiritual sensitivity to know the difference. But even then, when you have an impression to do good, it doesn't really matter that much where it came from. The following story illustrates this point.

Michelle D. Craig, currently a counselor in the Young Women general presidency, related the story of "Susan." Susan was the neighbor to President Spencer W. Kimball and a talented seamstress. Upon noticing President Kimball had a new suit, she decided to make him a tie. She sewed the tie, boxed it up and walked to his home. Before knocking on the door, she was filled with feelings of doubt, feeling presumptuous to give the prophet such a gift. Sister Craig continued the story: "Deciding she [Susan] had made a mistake, she turned to leave. Just then Sister Kimball opened the front door and said, 'Oh, Susan!' Stumbling all over herself, Susan said, 'I saw President Kimball in his new suit on Sunday. Dad just brought me some silk from New York ... and so I made him a tie.' Before Susan could continue, Sister Kimball stopped her, took hold of her shoulders, and said: 'Susan, never suppress a generous thought.'" [12]

Just as Sister Kimball counseled to "never suppress a generous thought," I believe we could apply the direction to "never suppress a righteous thought." We don't need to waste time wondering if the idea to help our neighbor came from the Holy Ghost or was just our own good thought; we should simply go and help. In truth, most good ideas are probably inspired by the Spirit anyway. As we strive to follow spiritual promptings without hesitation, we cultivate Christlike characteristics.

Eliminating pride and developing humility helps us develop spiritual resilience to manage times of doubt and discouragement. It also changes our character to become more like our Savior Jesus Christ.

Questions for self-reflection:

What can you do to decrease pride in your life?

What can you do to increase humility in your life?

How can you increase your sensitivity and obedience to spiritual promptings?

---

12 Michelle D. Craig, "Divine Discontent." *Ensign*, November 2018, 53.

CHAPTER EIGHT

"Is There One Among You Who Is Not Stripped of Envy?"

Alma the Younger's soul-searching questions continue as he asks, "Behold, I say, is there one among you who is not stripped of envy? I say unto you that such an one is not prepared; and I would that he should prepare quickly, for the hour is close at hand, and he knoweth not when the time shall come; for such an one is not found guiltless" (Alma 5:29).

Envy is considered one of the seven "deadly" sins. While it doesn't necessarily lead to physical death, it can contribute to ongoing spiritual death. Envy begins with comparison and can reduce gratitude. A person can have a very good life, but when they compare their situation to another, that same person can feel their life is less abundant. As gratitude decreases, entitlement increases, which leaves the individual unhappy and discontented.

We live in a world where comparison to others has never been more accessible. If we had lived two hundred years ago, I suppose we could have compared our farm to the next farm over, but opportunities to compare to others would have been scarce. I don't believe human nature has changed that much over time, and people have always been prone to rate themselves against others and be susceptible to envy. But current society allows you to see the varied circumstances of tens of thousands of others from the palm of your hand. If you personally struggle with envy, then this era of social media and instant communication may be particularly challenging.

It is natural to compare ourselves to others. When I say "natural," I mean it is part of our fallen natures and therefore something we need to eliminate. Some hear that a condition is "natural" and then presume it's acceptable. I don't feel that way. There are many human conditions that are quite natural but are evil and debased. One of the primary purposes of this life is to change our character from its base nature, or "natural" state, to an improved and more sanctified state. Quite simply, we are here to become like our Savior Jesus Christ.

Comparing ourselves to others seems to begin as we develop greater social awareness. I recall when this happened to me. When I began junior high school, I started the seventh grade feeling very much like a young kid. My interests were still quite juvenile, and I had minimal social understanding. I certainly paid little attention to my wardrobe and grooming. Yet in the eighth grade, something changed. I wanted to be clean and well-groomed. I thought more carefully about the clothing I wore. I noticed what others wore and wondered if my outfit would fit in. Above all, I wanted to change my haircut. Since birth I had a simple "bowl cut," with hair combed straight down. But as I began to notice other young men with cool hairstyles, I really wanted to part my hair. This happened at the beginning of my eighth-grade year. It seems like a pretty simple fix, right? I just needed to make the decision and change my hairstyle. But for me, it was not that easy.

For whatever reason, I greatly feared just showing up at school one day with a new hairstyle. I thought people would make fun of me for having one haircut the day before and then a new one the day after. It seems so silly now, especially since I have much less hair than I did then, but at the time it was very important. I really wanted to change my hairstyle but resisted due to fear of comparison. *I literally waited* until the summer between junior high school and high school to make the switch. I reasoned that I'd be less recognizable at high school, would potentially have a different peer group, and therefore be less vulnerable to comparison. I distinctly remember going to high school to get my schedule. My newly-styled hair was in place and I hoped I wouldn't see anyone I knew. Alas, I saw one of my female friends from junior high. She had known the straight-hair former me. Despite my attempts to avoid her, she saw me as we passed by. She smiled and said, "Nice haircut." Immediately my fears were gone. Had I been less worried about the perceptions of others and less prone to compare myself to them, my fears might have been absent in the first place.

Comparing ourselves to others can be a blessing and a curse. On the one hand, it can lead to increased motivation to change. On the other hand, it can lead to the sin of envy. Let's investigate both of these possible outcomes.

Sometimes we see what others have accomplished and this inspires us to become better. Perhaps you are currently in a career because of an encouraging mentor who had the same occupation. Aspiring youth look to sports stars and work extra hard to develop skills similar to their professional idols. Such individuals don't feel jealous of their heroes. They recognize the hard work those heroes put in to reach such excellence and then choose to do the same. Even in the gospel, we are encouraged to essentially compare ourselves to the Savior. We study His life, compare our characteristics to His, and change our lives to become like Him. We don't feel it is unfair that Jesus Christ has greater spirituality than we do. On the contrary, we see Him as a continuing source of inspiration and admiration. We know if we work hard, through His grace we can become like him. The type of comparison that leads to positive motivation and eager action is healthy and appropriate.

However, there is another side to comparison that leads to negative outcomes, particularly envy. At times we look at others and think, "They have such great lives! Their families are perfect, they take awesome vacations, and their hair always looks amazing." We then believe our lives are much worse in comparison, and feel envious of what these other people allegedly have. I say "allegedly" because there is often a fundamental flaw in our reasoning. The flaw is that we have usually based our decision on insufficient data to make an accurate conclusion. Social media proves this case in point.

Anymore, most of our comparison with others comes through social media. Social media is an amazing tool that helps us stay connected, share the gospel, and bless the lives of others. Of course, it can be used for inappropriate purposes as well, but I believe that it has greater positive than negative potential. Generally, when we post information on social media, we present the best of the best. I cannot remember the last time I posted a picture of my unmade bed, a dirty car, or a bad haircut. But I have posted many pictures of Disneyland trips, beach vacations, high school and college graduations, and the like. Even then, I don't post about the four-hour lines at Disneyland, or three hours of traffic I drove in to get to the coast. I post the great moments. I don't think there is anything wrong with people putting their best foot forward. The problem is when we compare our worst days to others' best days. When I compare my unmade bed to someone's Caribbean vacation, my life is certainly going to look worse in contrast. This type of comparison can lead to disappointment or discouragement, but when taken to a greater extreme, it leads to envy.

Envy is essentially competitive. It says, "Why should that person have such a good life? I work just as hard as they do, and I don't take amazing trips or have perpetually obedient children. It isn't fair that they have so much; I deserve that as well." This is a dangerous mindset. First, as previously discussed, it falsely presumes many conclusions about the lives of others. As they put their best lives forward, we do not see their suffering and failures. Second, this mindset suggests we are somehow less because someone has more. It supposes that we are in some sort of eternal race with others, and when someone moves ahead, that puts us at a disadvantage. Both of these assumptions fuel jealousy and envy that we could otherwise avoid.

Many are familiar with the parable of the prodigal son. A man had two sons. The first son was obedient and faithful, while the second son was impulsive and rash. The second son demanded his inheritance prematurely and received it. He promptly wasted it all, living the good life for a time. Can you imagine if he would have had access to social media? We would have seen his lavish lifestyle and thought, "Man, that guy has it all. Wouldn't it be great to live his life?" Yet his funds ran out and he was relegated to a scant living, working for a pig farmer. His life had become so desperate that as he fed the pigs, he wished he could join in their meal just to satisfy his own hunger. How things had changed since his days of extravagant living! Eventually the man humbled himself and determined to return to his father. He would not seek his former position as a cherished son but would beg to be a servant in his father's house, so at least he could get daily meals. I'm sure he was shocked when, upon his return, his father rejoiced. The son was treated with kindness and mercy. A large party commenced to celebrate the return of the wayward son.

On the day of the prodigal's return, the first son was working. No doubt he was on his father's errand. He had remained faithful throughout his brother's foolish antics. I'm sure he may have been tempted to request his inheritance right away as well, but he had the good sense to be patient, put in years of hard work, and receive the reward at the appropriate time. As this son returned from his labors, he heard merriment at his father's home. I'm sure he was curious; what was this about? He arrived to discover 1) his irresponsible brother had returned and 2) he had been received with celebration. The first son became angry and refused to enter the party.

The first son's reaction is very interesting. No doubt he felt very different that morning than he did once he discovered his miscreant brother was partying with friends with his father's approval. Just that morning he likely felt proud and satisfied with himself, but in the evening, he felt betrayed and envious. Yet very little in his life had changed throughout the day. His years of hard work were still in place. His long-standing obedience had not diminished. His loyalty to his father had not decreased. He had every reason to feel good about himself and appropriately proud of his accomplishments. Yet he sat there, angry and bitter. He was jealous that he never got a party. Note how his anger and bitterness only came *after* he compared his situation to his brother's. He let his brother's condition diminish his own achievements. That is a hard way to live. Someone is always going to be better than us, so if we let another's victory increase our feelings of defeat, we will experience much disappointment and frustration.

Elder Jeffery R. Holland stated: "Who is it that whispers so subtly in our ear that a gift given to another somehow diminishes the blessings we have received? Who makes us feel that if God is smiling on another, then He surely must somehow be frowning on us? You and I both know who does this—it is the father of all lies." [13] Envy convinces us that there is somehow a limited supply of heavenly blessings. If someone else gets one, then there is less for the rest of us. This is simply untrue. Satan would have us believe there is only room for one in the winner's circle. But in our journey back to heaven, there is enough space for all of us to win. Heavenly Father simply expands the winner's circle, making it larger and larger to include all who return through repentance and faithful keeping of covenants. Elder Holland further related: "I testify that no one of us is less treasured or cherished of God than another. I testify that He loves each of us—insecurities, anxieties, self-image, and all. He doesn't measure our talents or our looks; He doesn't measure our professions or our possessions. He cheers

---

13 Jeffrey R. Holland, "The Other Prodigal." *Ensign,* May 2002, https://www.lds.org/general-conference/2002/04/the-other-prodigal?lang=eng.

on *every* runner, calling out that the race is against sin, *not* against each other." [14]

Social media is not likely to go away. As a society we'll become more connected and be able to share more and more information. Opportunities for comparison and envy will only increase as time goes on. Eliminating envy can't be as simple as cutting ourselves off from social media. Remember, the brother of the prodigal son didn't have Twitter, and yet he was still envious. I believe there are some things we can do to eliminate envy from our lives.

Gratitude is an effective remedy for envy. We have so much to be grateful for. Sometimes we get caught up in the negative. As a psychologist I hear a lot of this. People don't typically come in for counseling because their lives are amazing. They come in distress, looking for ways to improve and feel less dejected. The first session usually consists of a recitation of everything that is wrong with their situation. In most cases, their reports are accurate. Their lives are rough and somewhat miserable. But I often find that their focus is a bit myopic, such that they are exclusively focused on the negative without acknowledging the positive. This would be like a criminal court case where only the prosecution was allowed to present evidence. If you were on a jury in such a case, you would probably convict the defendant. If all you heard was the arguments *against* the person, your decision would be easy. But a fair case would also involve arguments from the defense. As you listened to the evidence presented from both sides, you would have more to consider. You might even vote to acquit the defendant if you found the defense's evidence more compelling.

Putting excessive focus on the negative is like listening to a one-sided court case. It is unfair and results in biased conclusions. When your Instagram feed shows your friend's recent promotion and family vacation to Hawaii, you might be tempted to feel envious. This can be especially true if your current situation

---

14 Ibid.

includes a broken washing machine, a boss that doesn't appreciate your hard work, and the fact that your son got suspended *again* for arguing with his teacher. But as we try to think about the good, the bad often seems less by comparison. For example, perhaps you neglected to consider how your ministering brother is handy and can fix your washing machine. Or maybe you have not thought about how fortunate you are to have a job in the first place. Perhaps you have also forgotten how your son is a very good young man overall but has a temper that he is slowly learning to control. Focusing on such thoughts helps increase gratitude and temper envy.

When I was a full-time missionary in Mexico, I had a companion who was one of my favorites. We worked exceptionally well together, and our strong relationship yielded good results. One month we enjoyed very good success and saw many people join the church. We both felt extremely grateful for the Lord's mercy and blessings. We prayerfully thanked Him but felt there was more we could do to express our gratitude. We decided to fast for 24 hours. However, contrary to most fasts, we would not ask for anything. We would simply fast for gratitude, as a means of expressing our thankfulness to God. That was one of the most powerful fasts I have ever experienced. If you struggle with feelings of envy, remember gratitude as a helpful solution.

Another cure for envy is to rejoice in the successes of others. As previously discussed, envy is primarily competitive. When we pit ourselves against others, envy is a natural outcome. If you are racing against them, then every gain they make is a loss for you. But we need to remember that life was never designed to be competitive. We were put here to return to Father in Heaven, working out our individual salvation. We are here to help each other succeed. Satan has introduced the idea that we are in competition with each other as we return to our heavenly home. That idea is wrong and fuels inappropriate attitudes.

In The Church of Jesus Christ of Latter-day Saints, we make sacred covenants in holy temples. These covenants encourage us to respect and help others. Satan's answer to covenants is secret combinations. In a secret combination, there is only room for one at the top. It is highly competitive and constantly suspicious of the motivations of others. In the book of Ether, we read how the Jaredites adopted secret combinations that eventually led to their complete destruction. These started with Akish and the daughter of Jared, the king's daughter. Akish wanted to marry the daughter of Jared. When he approached King Jared to ask for her hand, Jared said he could marry his daughter in exchange for the murder of his future grandfather-in-law. Akish entered into a secret combination with his friends and together they conspired to kill the man. After marrying the daughter of Jared, Akish wanted the kingdom for himself. With the assistance of his secret combination, he beheaded his father-in-law, thus gaining control of the kingdom. As if this story isn't bad enough, Akish started to become jealous of his own son. Perhaps he thought that his son would follow in his dad's footsteps and start his own secret combination. Consequently, he incarcerated his *own son* and starved him to death. Akish was eventually murdered in a civil war that began with mutiny in his own family (see Ether chapters 8 and 9).

This story highlights how envy can lead to disastrous outcomes. Satan's plan says "take out everyone between you and first place; trip them and steal their running shoes. Do everything you can to eliminate the competition." The plan of salvation says "help those along the way. Give them your best shoes. We'll all cross the finish line at different times, but everyone has the potential to win." As we view life as a collaboration instead of a competition, feelings of envy naturally melt away.

Envy can also be alleviated as we develop greater self-confidence. I think that being jealous of others is often fueled by a belief that we are somehow insufficient. True self-confidence is in short supply in our society. I see many who appear self-assured but are simply covering insecurities with accolades and accomplishments. Those who are self-confident don't need a cheering section and a trophy shelf. They know who they are, what they are about, and are content to cheer on their fellow runners. I have a few friends that I believe are truly self-confident. They don't speak ill of others. I have never known them to be envious. I realize this evidence is anecdotal, but my experience leads me to believe that increasing feelings of self-confidence can help us see others in a different light.

True self-confidence comes from seeing ourselves as the Lord sees us. When we fail, the adversary tries to convince us we are worthless. Yet the Savior reaches out in compassion and understanding. Elder Dale G. Renlund of the Quorum of the Twelve Apostles explained this concept with an excellent and familiar example: "If Lucifer were teaching a child to walk and the child stumbled, he would scream at the child, punish him, and tell him to quit trying. Lucifer's ways bring discouragement and despair—eventually and always…. If Christ were teaching a child to walk and the child stumbled, He would help the child get up and encourage the next steps. Christ is the helper and consoler. His ways bring joy and hope—eventually and always." [15] Our Father in Heaven wants us to be successful and He understands our weakness. He is patient and understanding with our shortcomings. He views us in the glorious light of our divine potential and not in the discouraging shadow of our recent failures. As we adopt our Heavenly Father's perspective, we can become patient with ourselves. We will increase confidence in our own abilities notwithstanding our challenges. We won't need to envy others because we will be truly content with our own lives.

As we reduce feelings of jealousy and envy, our attitudes improve even though our situation might stay the same. Feelings of spiritual strength remain strong during times of difficulty. The future looks brighter and we will be more eager to help others

---

15 Dale G. Renlund, "Choose You This Day." *Ensign*, November 2018, 105.

instead of viewing them as our competitors. We will become more like the Savior who is the greatest cheerleader of all.

Questions for self-reflection:

How does comparing yourself to others impact your spirituality?

Consider how the Lord truly sees you, then compare that to your own self-perception. What can you do to see yourself as your Father in Heaven sees you?

If you were to increase feelings of gratitude in your life, how would that impact any existing feelings of envy or jealousy? What are some specific things you could be more grateful for?

CHAPTER NINE

"Is There One Among You That Doth Make a Mock of His Brother?"

Alma the Younger asks yet another question of the Zarahemla saints, stating, "And again I say unto you, is there one among you that doth make a mock of his brother, or that heapeth upon him persecutions? Wo unto such an one, for he is not prepared, and the time is at hand that he must repent or he cannot be saved!" (Alma 5:30-31).

Synonyms for mock include deride, jeer, or to treat with contempt. It sounds like the way one would treat an enemy as opposed to a friend. It reminds me of high school, where the standard for communication was often ridicule or sarcasm. Even among friends it was common to be the distributor or recipient of a biting remark or backhanded compliment. I see less of this among my peers as I grow older. Still, there is a concerning amount of negativity and persecution among us that can impact our spirituality and decrease our charity for others.

Alma asks whether there are any who "make a mock of their brother." Surely "brother" can refer to two groups; our spiritual siblings who include strangers and random associates, and those we consider close, including relatives, family members, and good friends. Let's consider both of these groups and how mockery and persecution can damage relationships and decrease spiritual power.

Unfortunately, it can be easy to "heap persecutions" upon those we do not know very well. Many of us can be quick to judge with very little information. I do this more often than I care to admit, especially when driving. I try to be efficient, including getting from place to place. Traffic makes me crazy, because I cannot figure out why traffic is slow. I think, "If everyone would just pay attention and focus on their driving, we could increase our overall speed." Sometimes I'll find there was an accident or road construction that slowed traffic, and in such cases I'm less perturbed. It's the *worst* when traffic is slow, then all of a sudden it just starts flowing again. I can't see any reason for the slowing except perhaps the poor driving habits of others. It makes me crazy. I know I need to learn to be more patient in such situations.

One time, I was particularly frustrated when driving. I was in a great hurry to reach my house. The road ahead was clear, and it seemed as if I would return home quickly. Then things changed. A car pulled out in front of me, not noticing my rapid rate of speed, and I slammed on the brakes. I was stuck behind this car and driving much slower than before. There was no way to pass the driver without breaking a number of laws. It seemed to me we were barely creeping down the road, but in reality, we were driving just a couple of miles per hour below the posted speed limit. In great frustration I rode that driver's tail, trying to send the message that they needed to get moving. It didn't work. Clearly, they didn't understand that I was in a hurry. Couldn't they understand my rush? Why didn't they speed up? My mind filled with thoughts of irritation towards this unknown person.

Finally, I was able to safely pass them. I made a point of staring in their direction as I did, casting a glare to effectively communicate my displeasure. What I saw changed my attitude in an instant. I didn't see an insensitive, careless or clueless driver.

Instead, I saw an elderly woman. She gripped the wheel tightly with both hands. Her face showed worry and concern. She did not look angry or insensitive. On the contrary, she looked vulnerable and scared. Perhaps she was frightened to drive at her age. Perhaps she was dealing with difficult life issues that consumed her thoughts. Perhaps she was scared by the maniac driver that had tailgated her for the past mile. At any rate, my feelings of hostility vanished and were replaced with contrition and shame. The Spirit gently rebuked me for my poor behavior. I drove the speed limit for the remainder of my trip.

Why does it seem so easy to judge others despite knowing so little about them? I don't believe I am alone in this practice. I see it constantly on the Internet, particularly in social media. Society has become polarized in political and social views, with opposing camps being very antagonistic. I find that people are often willing to be more hostile and critical toward those they are least familiar with. Sometimes we just have a single piece of information about a person, such as a certain political leaning or a position on a relevant social topic. Yet that solitary piece of data somehow leads us to render sweeping judgment regarding their personal lives, their intelligence, and their overall quality of character. As a social scientist, I can assure you that such judgment is absurd and almost universally incorrect. Single data points rarely provide enough information to yield correct conclusions. It seems to be part of our base, fallen natures to be critical of others.

In contrast, I have noticed an interesting pattern in my own life. The more information I have about someone else, the greater compassion I tend to feel for them. In my "angry driving" example, the faceless driver in front of me was the target of my wrath. All I knew about her was that she was driving slowly. But when I learned more about her, including the fact that she was elderly, scared, worried and nervous, my perception changed, and I felt greater empathy. I find that I have considerable patience for my close friends, children, parents, and extended family. It seems the more I know about them, the more I'm able to put their weaknesses into context and show greater compassion. Could it be that the more we know about someone, the greater potential we have to love and sustain them instead of mocking and persecuting them? The Savior's example suggests this is true.

Jesus Christ is the ultimate example of acceptance. Consider the following scriptures that describe His love and eternal longsuffering for us, His errant siblings:

"Nor height, nor depth, nor any other creature, shall be able to separate us from the love of God, which is in Christ Jesus our Lord." (Romans 8:39)

"For the mountains shall depart, and the hills be removed; but my kindness shall not depart from thee, neither shall the covenant of my peace be removed, saith the Lord that hath mercy on thee." (Isaiah 54:10)

I love the imagery in the Isaiah scripture. I live in the Pacific Northwest, surrounded by the beauty of nature, including massive mountains. There is a rest stop on a highway that I frequently travel. It marks the location where you can see the peaks of Mount Hood, Mount St. Helens, Mount Adams, and Mount Rainier all from one spot. Each peak is considerable in size, ranging from around 8,000 to over 14,000 feet in elevation. Reconsider the Savior's promise in Isaiah with the mountains in mind. "The mountains shall depart, and the hills be removed; but my kindness shall not depart from thee." In other words, you might wake up tomorrow and Mount Rainier could have vanished, and yet the Lord's love for you would still endure. The Savior always loves us, regardless of what we have done.

Now consider who knows us the best out of anyone. Would it be a spouse? A sibling? A close friend? Perhaps our mothers know us best. In each case we'd be wrong, because Jesus Christ understands us down to our most intimate and private characteristics. He sees all of our flaws, even those we strive to keep well hidden. He's even aware of things we have yet to discover about ourselves. God knows us perfectly and completely.

Let's combine these two qualities of the Savior and see what conclusion it yields. *The Lord Jesus Christ, who knows us the most, loves us the deepest.* Could it be that the more we come to know others, the greater acceptance and empathy we can have for them? If we resist the natural tendency to mock or judge others until we better understand their situation, a more righteous judgment will result. This concept appears to hold true in most relationships, with one puzzling exception.

I've found many are prone to "mock and heap persecution" upon siblings, parents, children and spouses without reservation. Sometimes when I am out in public, I am shocked to hear the way some parents talk to their children, or how certain spouses interact with each other. There is often so much hostility and aggression in their voices. I think to myself, "If that's the way they talk to each other in public, then what are they saying in private?"

Other times I see people who are not blatantly hostile but who speak with veiled sarcasm. I've read social media posts that say things like "Happy birthday to my numbskull husband" or "I love you to pieces even though you are sometimes an idiot." These people have gone to the trouble to publicly acknowledge their appreciation for someone they care about, but then add an element of sarcasm that is truly unnecessary. It's like making breakfast for someone, bringing it to them in bed, and then spitting in the orange juice on your way out. Why does this happen?

Sometimes we believe we can be sarcastic, demeaning or cruel to loved ones because of the perceived permanent nature of the relationship. We reason, "It's not like this person is going to leave me, so I can get in a few digs without losing any ground." I think both of those assumptions are incorrect. In the first place, there is no guarantee that relationships will last forever. Divorce is common. Families fall apart. Parents and children feud for decades without speaking to one another. If we think our closest relationships are somehow immune to decay, we are mistaken. They need to be nurtured and preserved just like any other relationship. In the second place, everything we do and say has an effect. Just because someone laughs at being called a dummy does not mean it did not hurt them. The cumulative effect of such comments can be destructive. I have seen it happen time and time again.

I believe personal sarcasm is a degree of emotional abuse. I'm not talking about sarcastic comments directed at situations, such as "I *love it* when it rains on our beach vacation" or "Waiting in gridlocked traffic is *my favorite thing.*" I'm talking about statements like "Oh yeah, I *love* my wife's cooking, especially when she burns everything and it tastes like cardboard," or "My husband is *so productive.* It's my favorite when he doesn't clean the garage for two years even though I've asked him to do it every weekend." There is no room for such communication in *any* relationship, particularly those we cherish most.

Another reason for sarcastic communication could be a lack of emotional intimacy. Emotional intimacy involves being emotionally close to and vulnerable with another person. It is *not* the same as sexual intimacy. It is quite possible to be sexually intimate without being emotionally intimate. Emotional intimacy is a characteristic of healthy relationships. It is where people can share, reveal, and discuss very sensitive topics without fear of ridicule or abandonment. This characteristic is quite difficult to develop and can require years and even decades of practice to master.

As a psychologist, I see many relationships, especially marriages, that lack emotional intimacy. With married couples I see people who genuinely love one another but are afraid to get truly close. They guard themselves with emotional suits of armor, for fear of being hurt. Sometimes they have been hurt in the past and are rightly wary of being hurt again. Other times they have been raised in families with no emotional intimacy and therefore have few examples to draw from. In any case, there is a distance between husband and wife caused by fear. In such relationships, I often see sarcastic communication. It's almost as if they are saying, "I really want to tell you how much I love you, but I'm afraid of getting hurt. I'll mix my love with a playful insult just to hedge my bets." A husband who feels this way might sarcastically say, "I'm glad I married you, but there are times when I have my doubts…" One of the biggest problems with this behavior is how it affects others. It can cause or deepen emotional rifts between the couple. When the other person hears the "loving insult," they think, "Well, it sounds like he loves me but perhaps not fully. How can I completely open up to someone who is partially closed off to me?" She then responds with her own sarcastic remark, such as, "It's not easy to love a dummy like you, but I make it work."

This type of communication damages relationships, yet we often do it. We falsely believe that little statements will not have significant effects. Alma's counsel to his son Helaman applies here: "By small and simple things are great things brought to pass" (Alma 37:6). The opposite applies as well; by "small and simple things" is great destruction brought to pass. Pulling a loose thread from a shirt may make no noticeable difference. But pulling a loose thread from a shirt *every day* will eventually reduce the shirt to nothing. It is a deception to believe that small, negative comments will not harm a relationship. In fact, they are doubly dangerous because 1) they have a powerful, cumulative effect and 2) because they are small, we are more inclined to justify and say them.

There is a simple solution to Alma the Younger's warning against mocking and persecuting others. It is this: be kind. Multiple, simple sarcastic statements can have a damaging effect over time. Conversely, making loving, caring comments can be a healing balm when applied consistently. It costs no money to be gentle. It takes little effort. Sometimes we must sacrifice pride, anger, or indignation to say a kind word, but those are things that should be discarded anyway. Kindness invites the Spirit into our lives and helps others feel the Spirit as well. Elder Joseph B. Wirthlin stated, "Kindness is the essence of a celestial life. Kindness is how a Christlike person treats others. Kindness should permeate all of our words and actions at work, at school, at church, and especially in our homes." [16] I like how he notes that kindness should be particularly prevalent in our homes. Our homes should be a refuge from hostility and unkindness, not the source of it.

Elder Wirthlin continued: "The things you say, the tone of your voice, the anger or calm of your words—these things are noticed by your children and by others. They see and learn both the kind and the unkind things we say or do. Nothing exposes our true selves more than how we treat one another in the home." [17] *Never underestimate* the power of your example, especially with those who look to you for guidance. Be aware that the things you say and do on a regular basis will have an effect on others. If you are unsure of just how kind or unkind you are from moment to moment, do a little experiment. Make a note of each kind or unkind thing you say on a daily basis. The frequency of either may surprise you, for good or for bad.

Finally, Elder Wirthlin addressed some common excuses: "'But,' you ask, 'what if people are rude?' Love them. 'If they are obnoxious?' Love them. 'But what if they offend? Surely I must do something then?' Love them. 'Wayward?' The answer is the same. Be kind. Love them." [18] In other words, there is no excuse. I can think of occasions when I have been unkind to others. Sometimes I believed my behavior was justified. Yet I have never looked back with satisfaction or pride on such moments. Alternatively, there are

---

16 Joseph B. Wirthlin, "The Virtue of Kindness." *Ensign,* May 2005, 26.
17 Joseph B. Wirthlin, "The Virtue of Kindness." *Ensign,* May 2005, 27.
18 Joseph B. Wirthlin, "The Virtue of Kindness." *Ensign,* May 2005, 28.

times I have shown kindness, whether or not the person deserved it. I have never regretted such decisions. Perhaps that is a gentle reminder to me, and maybe everyone, that we cannot go wrong being kind.

Examine your life and commit to be less sarcastic, less judgmental, and more kind. Doing so will help you maintain spiritual power. It will help sustain you spiritually and create a greater sense of peace and acceptance before the Lord.

Questions for self-reflection:

Have you been the recipient of harsh sarcasm? How did it make you feel? How do you suppose others feel when they receive the same treatment?

How would your judgments of others change if you saw them through the Savior's eyes?

What can you do to increase emotional intimacy in your most important relationships?

CHAPTER TEN

"Of What Fold Are Ye?"

In a seemingly irrelevant question to *members* of the church of Jesus Christ, Alma the Younger asks as follows: "And now if ye are not the sheep of the good shepherd, of what fold are ye?" (Alma 5:39). Wouldn't it go without saying that members of the church, admitted through baptism, belonged to the fold of the Savior? Alma clarifies his point:

> Behold, I say unto you, that the good shepherd doth call you; yea, and in his own name he doth call you, which is the name of Christ; and if ye will not hearken unto the voice of the good shepherd, to the name by which ye are called, behold, ye are not the sheep of the good shepherd…. Therefore, if a man bringeth forth good works he hearkeneth unto the voice of the good shepherd, and he doth follow him; but whosoever bringeth forth evil works, the same becometh a child of the devil, for he hearkeneth unto his voice, and doth follow him. (Alma 5:38,41)

Alma clarifies that one-time acts of righteousness, such as baptism and church admission, do not guarantee permanent placement in the fold of the Good Shepherd. By that same logic, it is reasonable that one-time acts of evil do not consign one to everlasting identification as a child of the devil. It seems this process is more complex than simple, at least to begin with. Another experience in Alma's life helps explain this concept.

Following his discourse in Zarahemla, Alma the Younger traveled to Ammonihah, preaching the gospel in order to reclaim wayward members of the church. He encountered an inactive church member named Amulek who became his "junior missionary" companion. Amulek was familiar with the gospel but clearly had been out of the game for a bit. The two of them joined together to preach to the people of Ammonihah. In the course of their teaching, they met a man named Zeezrom. Zeezrom was a lawyer but evidently a troublemaker at heart. The scriptures say he was "expert in the devices of the devil" (Alma 11:21). He asked if he could publicly question Amulek regarding a few issues. Amulek cautiously agreed. I've always wondered if Alma was a little worried about this proposition. It would be like a senior companion getting a brand new, inexperienced missionary and then sending her or him to teach an extremely antagonistic and knowledgeable investigator. Things could go poorly.

Zeezrom began his interrogation of Amulek with a brutish proposal: "Behold, here are six onties of silver, and all these will I give thee if thou wilt deny the existence of a Supreme Being" (Alma 11:22). Onties were part of Nephite currency, and based on Mormon's description of their value, six onties was probably worth a little more than a month's wages. This was no small sum. Still, I think it strange that Zeezrom simply attempted to bribe Amulek out of his testimony. Such strategies are rarely effective with the faithful.

Amulek refused to compromise his integrity for money, stating, "O thou child of hell, why tempt ye me? Knowest thou that the righteous yieldeth to no such temptations?" (Alma 11:23). Zeezrom continued to grill Amulek with doctrinal questions, attempting to confuse him and make him look foolish. Amulek answered strongly and ultimately bore down in pure testimony against Zeezrom. The power of true doctrine, fortified by the witness of the Holy Ghost, was easily more potent than Zeezrom's mortal reasoning. "Now, when Amulek had finished these words the people began again to be astonished, and also Zeezrom began to tremble" (Alma 11:46).

As Zeezrom trembled, Alma began teaching. Perhaps for the first time in his life, Zeezrom sincerely listened to the words of a prophet. The instruction of Alma and Amulek caused him to believe, or maybe return to believe, in true doctrine. But his previous efforts to incite the people against Alma and Amulek were quite effective. What followed was tragic. Alma and Amulek were imprisoned. Faithful women and children were burned alive for their beliefs. Zeezrom tried to undo his former actions, pleading with the leaders to stop their madness. It was to no avail, and Zeezrom was cast out by those who sought to kill him. Ultimately, Alma and Amulek were miraculously delivered from bondage and the entire city of Ammonihah was destroyed in a single day (see Alma 16:9-11).

Zeezrom escaped to a neighboring city where he fell very ill, consumed with guilt. He believed Alma and Amulek had perished and that he was to blame, so truly his feelings had merit. When Zeezrom learned they had survived, he sent for them. They came to his bedside to find a humble, repentant man, very different from the man they contended with a few days prior. Alma gave him a blessing of healing. Based on his humility and faith in Jesus Christ, Zeezrom immediately recovered and spent subsequent years being a faithful missionary companion to Alma and Amulek. It is a very happy ending to what could have otherwise been a great misfortune.

Going back to Alma the Younger's original discussion regarding the Good Shepherd (see Alma 5:38,41), was Zeezrom a member of Christ's fold or was he a child of the devil? I think most people would say the answer is not simple. When he was actively tempting Amulek and trying to destroy missionary work, it seems he was obeying Lucifer. When he was repentant and trying to undo the damage he caused, he was obeying the Savior. As far as we know, Zeezrom stayed faithful and most likely remained in the fold of the Good Shepherd. But what if later in life he returned to his old, disobedient ways? If that were the case, then one could argue he was back in the devil's camp. We simply do not know.

Fortunately, it is not up to us to evaluate such issues. Jesus Christ, our loving and righteous Judge, will ensure all judgment is done with justice and mercy. Yet the implications of Alma's teachings and Zeezrom's history are critical for us on an individual level. We have to decide, every day, if we are going to be in the fold of the Good Shepherd or the fold of the devil. The manifestation of these decisions come through our works. Remember Alma the Younger's instruction: "If a man *bringeth forth good works* he hearkeneth unto the voice of the good shepherd, and he doth follow him; but *whosoever bringeth forth evil works*, the same becometh a child of the devil, for he hearkeneth unto his voice, and doth follow him" (Alma 5:41, emphasis added). Sometimes the decision to choose good works is easy. Other times it can be very difficult.

I remember being taught as a youth to just "decide once" to be righteous, so that when you are tempted, you won't make a bad decision. I like that concept, but it hasn't always worked for me. For example, when I was in seminary, we had a lesson on the Word of Wisdom. I made the initial choice that I would never use any of the prohibited substances. I've never had to make that decision again, because I am not remotely tempted to break that commandment. For whatever reason, substance abuse does not entice me. Because of that, I'm not bothered by temptations to use drugs or alcohol. In fact, I think that Lucifer has probably given up in that area and eliminated substance abuse from my personalized temptation plan. Clearly, when it comes to the Word of Wisdom, I'm in the Savior's fold.

However, I also remember having lessons in seminary about not judging others unrighteously. With youthful zeal, I made the initial decision that I would never make hasty and vain judgments about others. I would follow the Lord's example and treat them with kindness and dignity. In opposite experience to my Word of Wisdom endeavors, I have since found that it is often quite difficult for me to withhold judgment. Just as some may be enticed by a cold beer, I'm tempted with the urge to be critical or disparaging. I don't doubt my original sincerity when I committed to follow the Savior's example of righteous judgment. I have just found it very, very difficult to follow through with my commitment. In fact, I find that I have to recommit to keep this commandment over and over again. Sometimes I am obedient but often I'm not. It is an ongoing process and surely the "decide once" decision was insufficient for me to beat this vice. I'm certain Lucifer has underlined and bolded "unrighteous judgment" in my personalized temptation plan. When it comes to this issue, am I in the Savior's fold or the devil's?

I think the answer to that question is complex. When I'm obedient to the commandments, I believe I'm one of the Lord's sheep. When I'm being disobedient, I believe I'm following Satan's flock. It's like I've constructed a bridge between the tree of life and the great and spacious building and traveling back and forth. Due to our fallen natures, I think my experience may be familiar to many. Most of us can think of areas where we struggle to be obedient. We leave church on Sunday with a renewed determination to do well. During the week we yield to temptation and commit sin. We go to Father in Heaven, again and again, with godly sorrow and a sincere desire to change. We return to church the following Sunday, humbly intending to renew our covenants of obedience and redouble our efforts. This becomes an iterative process that, if performed successfully, can ultimately result in our exaltation. But it is usually not a one-time decision, and it doesn't mean that once we've determined to sell our stake in the great and spacious building that we never return for a visit.

The cumulative effect of millions of choices will eventually determine our placement in the Savior's fold or the devil's flock. C. A. Hall said, "We sow our thoughts, and we reap our actions; we sow our actions, and we reap our habits; we sow our habits, and we reap our characters; we sow our characters, and we reap our destiny." [19] In my experience, this quote is accurate. It describes the progression that begins with simple, passing thoughts and ends with ultimate outcomes that may be unchangeable. I have seen it happen over and over. Through choice after choice we develop character traits that are difficult to change. This is both good and bad news, because the process holds equally true for righteous choices and evil decisions. For each of us, our characters are currently being shaped, choice by choice.

Brad Wilcox tells the story of a troubled young man who made chronically poor decisions. Brother Wilcox reasoned that if they could get the boy to Especially for Youth (EFY), which was like a spiritual summer camp for teenagers, perhaps this could help improve his behavior. Although they were able to get him to the program, Brother Wilcox described the outcome: "We finally got the kid to EFY, but how long do you think he lasted? Not even a day. By the end of the first day he called his mother and said, 'Get me out of here!' Heaven will not be heaven for those who have not chosen to be heavenly." [20]

Brother Wilcox's conclusion that "heaven will not be heaven for those who have not chosen to be heavenly" is true and supported by scripture. In Doctrine and Covenants 88, the Lord talks about the three degrees of glory. Even though the highest degree is the most desirable, He indicates there are some who will simply not want to be there. "And they who remain shall also be quickened; nevertheless, they shall return again to their own place, *to enjoy that*

---

19 C.A. Hall, *The Home Book of Quotations* (New York, Dodd, Mead and Company, 1935) 845.

20 Brad W. Wilcox, "His Grace is Sufficient." *BYU Speeches*, https://speeches.byu.edu/talks/brad-wilcox_his-grace-is-sufficient/. Accessed 5 June 2019.

which they are willing to receive, because they were not willing to enjoy that which they might have received. *For what doth it profit a man if a gift is bestowed upon him, and he receive not the gift?* Behold, he rejoices not in that which is given unto him, neither rejoices in him who is the giver of the gift" (D&C 88:32-33, emphasis added). In other words, what good would it do to drag a young man to EFY when he never wanted to go there in the first place? What blessing would it be to force a man to the celestial kingdom if he had forged a terrestrial character throughout life? He would much prefer to be among those like himself. Although we should always invite people to do good and seek righteousness, in the end we cannot and should not attempt to force them towards any particular result. In the eternal outcome, it sounds like we will eventually find our way back to where we feel most comfortable.

However, for those of us who have made sacred covenants with God, the decision should be clear. We should choose to become the sort of people who will feel quite comfortable in Father in Heaven's presence. For those who have yet to make such covenants, the Lord's missionaries work on both sides of the veil to bring them to the truth. I believe most of us loved our Father in Heaven deeply before we left His presence. We wanted nothing more than to return to be with Him. Although we do not recall our former feelings, much of this life is designed to help us remember and reignite our desire to do whatever it takes to be with Him again. The celestial kingdom should be our singular goal, which means we need to be firmly fixed in the fold of God.

So, what do we do? Simply declaring our desire to be part of the Savior's fold is important but insufficient. Jesus taught that those who hear His words but fail to act are built upon sand and will fall when adversity strikes. Only those who hear His words *and* do them create a solid foundation that will sustain them through difficulties (see Matthew 7:24-27). Reemphasizing the same principle, Alma said, "If a man *bringeth forth good works* he hearkeneth unto the voice of the good shepherd, and he doth follow him" (Alma 5:41, emphasis added). Good works are critical. *Daily* good works are essential. Satan tries to convince us that missing a single prayer, avoiding a church meeting, or postponing a temple visit is not a big deal. Believe me, *the very fact* that Satan is trying to influence you means it *is* a big deal. He wants us to fail and be miserable. I don't think he cares if our misery comes from one colossally bad decision or the cumulative effect of one thousand small choices, as long as we are ultimately unhappy. Don't fall for the trap that small decisions are not important. *Every decision related to our salvation* is important. We should intentionally choose the right as often as we can, and then sincerely repent when we choose poorly.

For generations we have been taught to develop a habit of regular spiritual practices, such as daily prayer, daily scripture study, weekly partaking of the sacrament, and regular temple attendance. Let's briefly address each of these familiar practices:

Prayer

Prayer is our connection to God and is available to anyone. The eloquent and illiterate are heard equally. We are commanded to "pray always" (2 Nephi 32:9), suggesting prayerful habits should be consistent. When I was a full-time missionary, I felt the companionship of the Spirit throughout the day. It seemed like even our moment-to-moment decisions were divinely directed. After I returned home and was no longer a full-time missionary, I didn't feel the same spiritual closeness to God. I figured it was because I no longer wore the black missionary nametag. Then I started to wonder if my assumption was correct. I reflected on how, as a missionary, I would pray upwards of twenty to thirty times per day. I prayed with others. I prayed on my own. I prayed for help. I prayed for direction. Now that I was home, I was praying maybe twice every day. I began to think there was less magic in the black nametag than I had supposed, and perhaps the reason I felt the

Spirit less was because my prayer frequency had reduced by at *least* a factor of ten.

Prayer is a tremendous opportunity. Sister Carol F. McConkie, a former counselor in the Young Women general presidency, stated, "Prayer is a gift from God. We need never feel lost or alone. I testify that every moment of precious prayer can be holy time spent with our Father, in the name of the Son, by the power of the Holy Ghost." [21] Ensure you make prayer a significant priority in your life.

Scripture study

The scriptures are available because of great personal struggle to many who have gone before us. I think of Nephi retrieving the brass plates, Ether risking his life to document his people's civil war, and Moroni hiding from murderous Lamanites as he recorded the tragic end of his beloved nation. Countless others sacrificed time and effort to record and preserve the words of God for the benefit of future generations. We are that future generation and owe our forebears a profound debt of gratitude.

I remember being very excited to get my first set of scriptures. They were leather-bound with my name engraved in gold. They were expensive and I was grateful to my parents for making the sacrifice to obtain them. But, back then, not everyone had the resources or ability to have such a lovely set of scriptures. Times have changed. Today, if you have a cell phone, one minute, and a decent internet connection, you can get a *free* copy of the Gospel Library app. This app contains all the scriptures, thousands of pictures, decades of General Conference talks, the *Come, Follow Me* curriculum, manuals, handbooks, and many other resources that will bless your life. Most everyone can now access the scriptures on a regular basis.

---

21 Carol F. McConkie, "The Soul's Sincere Desire." *Ensign*, November 2016, 27.

Elder Richard G. Scott stated, "Scriptures are like packets of light that illuminate our minds and give place to guidance and inspiration from on high. They can become the key to open the channel to communion with our Father in Heaven and His Beloved Son, Jesus Christ." [22] We should make time to study the scriptures on a daily basis. Doing so will bring the Spirit into our lives and help us be strong through moments of doubt and discouragement.

Partaking of the sacrament

The sacrament is the only ordinance that Latter-day Saints partake of, for themselves, on a recurring basis. It incorporates the physical act of eating and drinking to help us consciously remember and recommit to sacred covenants. I believe most active members of the church partake of the sacrament on a regular basis. But I also believe that many active members, including myself, could benefit from greater personal preparation to participate in this holy ordinance. In a recent church meeting, we discussed strategies to increase reverence during the sacrament service. The question came up as to when we should begin to prepare ourselves to receive the sacrament. I remember thinking, "We should never *stop* preparing to take the sacrament, spending our entire week focusing on the upcoming ordinance." As we promise to "always remember Him" (D&C 20:77), we can better fulfill that agreement by thinking of Him more frequently and preparing to formally remember Him, through the sacrament, more intentionally.

Elder Jeffrey R. Holland stated, "The sacrament of the Lord's Supper [is] the sacred, acknowledged focal point of our weekly worship experience. We are to remember in as personal a way as possible that Christ died from a heart broken by shouldering entirely alone the sins and sorrows of the whole human family.

---

22 Richard G. Scott, "The Power of Scripture." *Ensign*, November 2011, 6.

Inasmuch as we contributed to that fatal burden, such a moment demands our respect."[23] Amen to that.

Temple attendance

When my parents were children, they were invited to memorize and recite the location of each temple throughout the world. There were ten temples at the time, making the task relatively easy. You'd have to be somewhat of a prodigy to do the same task today. Including temples that have been dedicated, are under construction, or have been announced, they number more than two hundred. In 2014, Elder Quentin W. Cook, a member of the Quorum of the Twelve Apostles, reported that more than 85% of members of the church lived within 200 miles of a temple. I'm guessing that percentage has increased over time and will continue to increase, especially considering the announcements of temples in such locations as Thailand, Cambodia, Guam, Dubai, and Russia.

Temple attendance will always require a sacrifice, but the sacrifice of time, travel and means is becoming less and less. Going to the house of the Lord is one of the greatest blessings afforded to Latter-day Saints. Some years ago, I was at the Portland Oregon temple with a group of youth. The temple president spoke with them. He remarked how his friends had recently traveled to Jerusalem. They told of the thrill they had as they traveled the same roads where Jesus had literally been some two thousand years ago. They said it was amazing to have "walked where Jesus walked." Then the president looked intently at the youth and said, "When you come to this temple, you have walked where Jesus walked. This is His house. He comes here personally and walks these halls. You don't need to travel to Jerusalem to walk where

---

23 Jeffrey R. Holland, "Behold the Lamb of God." *Ensign*, May 2019, 45.

He walked; you just have to come here." It was a powerful spiritual moment and the Spirit testified to me that it was true.

President Thomas S. Monson stated, "As I think of temples, my thoughts turn to the many blessings we receive therein. As we enter through the doors of the temple, we leave behind us the distractions and confusion of the world. Inside this sacred sanctuary, we find beauty and order. There is rest for our souls and a respite from the cares of our lives." [24] Do you want rest for your soul? Do you want respite from life's challenges? Make the needed sacrifices to qualify to enter the house of the Lord and then attend regularly.

Life will necessarily have its ups and downs. We can maintain greater strength during times of discouragement as we faithfully implement these simple principles. This will help us secure our position in the fold of God and forge eternal characters that will make us want to be with Him again.

Questions for self-reflection:

What commandments are difficult for you to keep? What can you do to increase your commitment to be obedient in these areas?

How can you improve habits of prayer, scripture study and temple attendance?

What can you do to better prepare to partake of the sacrament on a weekly basis?

---

24 Thomas S. Monson, "Blessings of the Temple." *Ensign*, May 2015, 91.

CHAPTER ELEVEN

"I Know These Things of Myself"

One of Alma the Younger's final questions to the Zarahemla saints related to his own testimony: "Do ye not suppose that I know of these things myself? Behold, I testify unto you that I do know that these things whereof I have spoken are true. And how do ye suppose that I know of their surety? Behold, I say unto you they are made known unto me by the Holy Spirit of God" (Alma 5:45-46). We discussed earlier how having a testimony and being converted are two different things. Testimony involves receiving a witness of the truth and is a necessary first step for conversion. Conversion includes ongoing action based on the truth of testimony, developing strong gospel roots. Not everyone who receives a testimony becomes converted.

Consider the example of Peter. We know he had a testimony of Jesus Christ, as related in Matthew chapter 16. Peter bore witness of the Savior's divinity, and the Savior confirmed that his testimony had come from God and not man. Peter's conviction was sincere, but like the rest of us, he was weak and vulnerable to temptation. Following the Savior's arrest, Peter kept a cautious distance, curious to see what would happen. As he kept his watch, he was identified by three separate people as being an associate of Jesus. For reasons unknown, Peter denied knowing the Lord. "And immediately, while [Peter] yet spake, the cock crew. And the Lord turned, and looked upon Peter. And Peter remembered the word of the Lord, how he had said unto him, Before the cock crow, thou shalt deny me thrice. And Peter went out, and wept bitterly" (Luke 22:60-62).

The aforementioned events had been prophesied by the Lord during the Last Supper. Although Peter claimed he would follow the Savior anywhere, even unto death, the Lord essentially told him that he was not yet strong enough. "And the Lord said, Simon, Simon, behold, Satan hath desired to have you, that he may sift you as wheat: But I have prayed for thee, that thy faith fail not: *and when thou art converted, strengthen thy brethren*" (Luke 22:31-32, emphasis added). Peter already had a testimony, but he was not yet converted. In time, his conversion was complete, and he became one of the strongest advocates of the risen Lord.

The parable of the sower can help us understand the relationship between testimony and conversion. It is one of the few parables that Jesus gave *and* personally explained its meaning. In this parable (see Matthew 13), the Lord describes a man who went forward with seeds, spreading them in hopes they would grow. The seeds landed in many different settings. Some fell along the side of the road. Some fell in stony places. Some fell among thorns. Yet others fell into good ground. The Lord then explained that the seed was the word of God. The following paragraphs detail His explanation of the various circumstances in the parable.

Falling by the wayside: "When any one heareth the word of the kingdom, and understandeth *it* not, then cometh the wicked *one*, and catcheth away that which was sown in his heart. This is he which received seed by the way side" (Matthew 13:19). These are those who hear the word of God. The word is desirable and is "sown in his heart." But they lack sufficient understanding to keep the desire alive. Doubts arise and their tender testimony is devoured, leaving no basis for belief. Conversion is impossible because testimony is absent.

Stony places: "But he that received the seed into stony places, the same is he that heareth the word, and anon with joy receiveth it; Yet hath he not root in himself, but dureth for a while: for when tribulation or persecution ariseth because of the word, by and by he is offended" (Matthew 13:20-21). These are those who not only hear the word, but happily receive it. Perhaps there are gospel truths that resonate with them. Perhaps they derive strength from the strong testimonies of others, such as good friends or full-time missionaries. But when difficulties begin and choices must be made, the person is ultimately offended and loses interest. There is not enough root to preserve their belief. Conversion is thwarted as the root of testimony dies.

Among the thorns: "He also that received seed among the thorns is he that heareth the word; and the care of this world, and the deceitfulness of riches, choke the word, and he becometh unfruitful" (Matthew 13:22). Here we have those that hear the word, want to believe, and may even get the beginnings of testimony. But things start to get in the way of belief. The "cares of the world" can be anything that distract us from faithful obedience. Wealth is specifically listed as a potential distraction. Although money has great potential to bless others, it can also become a hinderance if it becomes a primary focus. Those among the thorns have their testimonies choked and obstructed, leaving no possibility for growth into conversion.

Good ground: "But he that received seed into the good ground is he that heareth the word, and understandeth it; which also beareth fruit, and bringeth forth, some an hundredfold, some sixty, some thirty" (Matthew 13:23). These individuals hear and receive the word. Furthermore, they *understand* it. They seek answers to their questions and rely on the Lord for knowledge. In addition, they *bear fruit*. Fruit does not generally come from seeds that are haphazardly scattered in the soil. It comes from seeds that are intentionally planted and cultivated. This takes time and ongoing effort. Those who nurture their seeds, growing them into plants of testimony, eventually yield the fruit of conversion.

In my opinion, the ongoing companionship of the Holy Ghost is the best way to transform the tender twig of testimony into the colossal evergreen of conversion. These towering trees are highly resilient to doubts, fears, detractors, and other potential threats. Their deep roots sustain the believer through all sorts of questions and concerns. We know that those who have the gift of the Holy Ghost have the promise they can *always* have the Spirit with them, upon conditions of obedience. Making continuous righteous choices is an excellent strategy to maintain the company of the Holy Ghost.

In 2018 President Russell M. Nelson provided a warning to the world. I remember listening to this talk and feeling the Spirit telling me to pay particular attention to what was being said. President Nelson stated, "In coming days, it will not be possible to survive spiritually without the guiding, directing, comforting, and constant influence of the Holy Ghost." [25] I went back and re-read his remarks. "It will not be possible to survive spiritually." He didn't say it seems unlikely, or there's a chance that you won't survive. The prophet of the Lord said that, in days not far hence, "it will not be possible" to spiritually survive without the sustaining companionship of the Holy Ghost. I take prophetic warnings seriously. I think everyone should. President Nelson essentially says there are many "wayside places, stony places, and thorns" out there. If we don't protect and nurture our testimonies with the Spirit, they are likely to die.

Our world is filled with deceptive voices. Such voices now have global reach like never before. Antichrists of yesteryear could only preach to local congregations. Korihor, a Book of Mormon antichrist, had many followers but his overall reach was limited. If he were around today, he'd have a website that is search engine optimized, massive email marketing, and a YouTube channel with millions of views. Although the truth has never had a bigger

---

25 Russell M. Nelson, "Revelation for the Church, Revelation for Our Lives" *Ensign*, May 2018, 96.

platform, lies have a megaphone just as large. We need revelation from the ultimate source of truth in order to filter out deception and preserve our testimonies.

In the same April 2018 address, President Nelson made another statement that impressed me deeply. He proclaimed, "Nothing opens the heavens quite like the combination of increased purity, exact obedience, earnest seeking, daily feasting on the words of Christ in the Book of Mormon, and regular time committed to temple and family history work." [26] To me, that almost sounds like a recipe for revelation. I invite you to give careful consideration to each item he discussed. Here are some questions that can facilitate your reflection:

What does it mean to you to be pure? What areas of your life are currently impure? What can you do to increase personal purity?

Why is obedience essential? What is the difference between obedience and exact obedience? What are some areas in your life where increased obedience would yield greater blessings?

What do you currently seek? What does it mean to be earnest when we seek? What things would the Lord have you seek for, and are those different from your current goals?

How often do you read the Book of Mormon? What is the difference between reading, studying, and feasting on the words of scripture?

How much time do you commit to temple attendance and family history work? What things in life can you eliminate or reduce in order to increase the time you devote to this critical practice?

My beloved brothers and sisters, the joy of the gospel is there for all. Active participation in The Church of Jesus Christ of Latter-

---

26 Russell M. Nelson, "Revelation for the Church, Revelation for Our Lives." *Ensign*, May 2018, 95.

day Saints yields great satisfaction. Trials and disappointments will come, but they can be tempered by faithful adherence to covenants. Satan's influence on you can be reduced to practically zero as you strive to keep the Holy Ghost with you at all times. Remember Alma the Younger's essential question: "And now behold, I say unto you, my brethren, if ye have experienced a change of heart, and if ye have felt to sing the song of redeeming love, I would ask, can ye feel so now?" (Alma 5:26).

Changes of heart are waiting. The song of redeeming love is composed, and choirs of angels are ready to join in the chorus. *Yet we have to choose to sing.* In addition, we have to remember the times we've sung in the past. We need to make the daily choices that will help us not only recall past spiritual successes but achieve ongoing spiritual power. May we ever prepare for that blessed time when the song of redeeming love will be our constant refrain: "And he hath brought to pass the redemption of the world, whereby he that is found guiltless before him at the judgment day hath it given unto him to dwell in the presence of God in his kingdom, to sing ceaseless praises with the choirs above, unto the Father, and unto the Son, and unto the Holy Ghost, which are one God, in a state of happiness which hath no end" (Mormon 7:7). God bless us all to look forward to that remarkable day.

ABOUT THE AUTHOR

David T. Morgan is a licensed psychologist with over twenty years of experience in the mental health field. He has a B.S. in psychology, an M.S. in counseling and guidance, and a Ph.D. in counseling psychology, all from Brigham Young University. He is the author of *My God Hath Been My Support: Seven Keys to Understanding and Enduring Personal Trials, Peace Be Unto You: Anxiety Management Using Gospel Principles,* and *Peace Be Unto You: Anxiety Management Using Gospel Principles: Individual Workbook.* He and his amazing wife are the parents of six children and grandparents of three. David is a lover of the scriptures and truly believes the answers to life's challenges can be found in the words of ancient and modern prophets. He also loves Disneyland and knows almost more about the Happiest Place on Earth than he does about psychology.

www.ldspsychologist.com

Made in the USA
Middletown, DE
14 August 2020